Alison Allan

Carry On Heavenly

The book was printed digitally on-demand.

Printed in the European Union on environmentally friendly, chlorine- and acid-free paper.

The author is responsible for the content and correction.

© 2016 united p. c. publisher

ISBN 978-3-7103-2627-1
Cover photo: Alison Allan
Cover design, layout & typesetting: united p. c. publisher

www.united-pc.eu

Contents

Foreword by Kari Mena 7
Introduction 9
Chapter 1: The Carry On Team 13
Chapter 2: Kenneth Williams 20
Chapter 3: Joan Sims and the Team 40
Chapter 4: Bernard Bresslaw 50
Chapter 5: Bernard the Love Guru 57
Chapter 6: Sid James 61
Chapter 7: Charles Hawtrey and the Team 68
Chapter 8: Bernard Explores the Afterlife 72
Chapter 9: Peter Rogers 81
Chapter 10: Back to Bernard 87
Chapter 11: Joan Sims 95
Chapter 12: Kenneth Connor –
Life was a Blessing 100
Chapter 13: Kenny Williams
and Frankie Howerd 102
Chapter 14: Gerald Thomas, Director 112
Chapter 15: Hattie Jacques 129
Chapter 16: Talbot Rothwell,
A Last Minute Visit 135
Chapter 17: Goodbye,
Carry On Heavenly Team 139

Foreword by Kari Mena

I've been invited by my best girl Alison to write the foreword to her latest book, Carry On Heavenly. "And I'll need it by the end of the week, right. Brilliant. Thanks Babes." One week! I hadn't finished a book in over two years and now I had to read a whole book in a matter of days AND write something spectacular about it. Still, I was up for the challenge and very honoured for the opportunity.

I started reading right away and then I couldn't stop. Sure, I had a short deadline, but it was the content that kept me glued to its pages. I had never heard of the show Carry On and didn't know any of the players but their personalities came right through and I found them all to be very charming. Those that are fans will find the interaction and reminiscing of old friends delightful. The fun doesn't stop there though. These pages are packed with one of a kind insights from across the veil. Some passages are so informative and validating that I was brought to tears. Others are mind blowing and had me staring wide-eyed and jaw-dropped in amazement.

The topics discussed, from self-love to quantum entanglement, come from the perspective of those that have the benefit of easily accessing knowledge from the spirit world, knowledge that we here on earth find so elusive. During these discussions, the cast retain their comedic and bantering personalities, making everything feel light and entertaining, yet remaining both obviously and covertly insightful.

Alison is a beacon to those on both sides and a gift to everyone who has ever had the pleasure to know her. It is clear in her interactions with the Carry On family that they have become very fond of her, and her them. I can vouch for that exchange; once I connect with a spirit, I feel love and gratitude for them that I'll carry with me until I meet up with them back Home, until I Carry On Heavenly. Alison's talent for writing and her knowledge of the metaphysical combined with her mediumship skills all play a part in this illuminating and fascinating account of a soul family reunited on the flip side.

Introduction

I have been channelling interviews for just over a year now since my gifts opened up to the spirit world. I have always been sensitive to spirits but in the last few years my gifts have really let loose. My life is very much filled with spiritual activity from interviews of the crossed over, to readings for those that haven't, and a great deal more. I am still developing these gifts and learning confidence with them which is not easy in the type of world we live in where everything has to be evidence based or it's laughed at as folly or worse – mental health issues. So it takes great personal dedication and strength to deal with that mindset and come out into the psychic playground. This is such an occasion.

When Hattie Jacques showed up several months ago I was thrilled to be able to interview her and it was my first experience where more than one famous spirit came through at the same time; she brought Erik Sykes with her. Prior to this I had met Frankie Howerd but struggled to make a good connection to him as he can be a bit of a mystery, so I thought he was just popping in for a chat like some of them do. For mediums these events are quite normal – they talk to famous spirits all the time, usually the ones they felt a strong love for in their lives; but perhaps what isn't normal is the level to which the spirit world is now looking to be channelled by the three-Dimensional world more publicly.

I never imagined that a couple of months later the greater part of the Carry On Team would drop by and give me such a long interview – long enough to publish in book form. Here I should mention that it's a combination of both my spirit team which includes Erik Medhus from Channelling Erik, my Dad, Al Capone (*through a recent interview he became part of my spirit team*), my sister Helen who crossed at seven months gestation and many more that help bring these spirits to me in the first place, along with my own openness to connect with them and that everyone is accessible in spirit if they so choose it and I mean everyone – the only shortcoming in channelling is one's own inhibitions.

I feel very blessed by this channelled work. The Carry On Team filled my life with love and laughter every day for several months in the latter half of 2015 until they decided it was time to let me complete the project. Spirits have freewill and will only do what they want to. They can't be coerced like humans can and they can see the bigger picture of what's to come. I discovered that each of the cast of Carry On was so unique, and had so much wisdom to offer. Their musings were very interesting and I learned a great deal about their lives and the spirit world from them. They were patient with me and took the time to find out about who I am in the process – they spent time with my dad, read my other books, commented on my artworks and most of all, answered my insane questions about the afterlife. So was born *Carry On Heavenly*.

A brief word on channelling – it is fraught with challenges. The channellers, for a start, are interpreting information coming from all manner of ways through a higher dimensional plane such as, knowing, feeling, hearing and seeing, and we often aren't sure of ourselves in the process. (*This has a lot to do with society being proof-based, proof then belief but the opposite is actually true. Abraham-Hicks are a great source of information on that subject.*)

As channellers, we know we're getting information from the spirit world but we can't always verify it to satisfy that proof-first notion and so I will often ask for extra things from the spirits I'm interviewing just to doubly confirm what I'm receiving, and who I'm receiving it from. I get visitors both in the room with me and in my third eye. Without stepping into mistrust of the process and one's own self-doubt too much, it's better to be sure of who you're talking to than not – not all spirits are good spirits and so assuring yourself you're working with only what is for your highest good is a damn good thing. Just like you wouldn't cross a busy road without looking – checking your instincts are correct before diving into channelling is quality astral road-safety.

Further to this – information doesn't come like a written letter or a phone call and psychics don't get to know everything – imagine that you have to wear glasses to see properly (*some of you already are right now*) and that's just in this dimension; you haven't even crossed the veil yet – well – from here you can see the analogy is that crossing the veil to communicate is not the same as talking to your neighbour one on one with your specs on, nor is it like hearing a crystal clear phone call. Clairaudient gifts or clear hearing is great – those types of psychics get so much more information and more accurate too. I am an intuitive medium which gives me a bit of everything so I have to work quite hard to interpret from grainy pictures, to words, to knowings – it's a bit like riding a bike while cleaning your teeth and feeding the cat! So on that note – I hope you enjoy my interpretations of the wonderful images, words, feelings, and knowings that this amazing team of spirits gave me so we can all Carry On Heavenly...

Chapter 1: The Carry On Team

This started out as my normal style of interview that I do with a spirit. Kenneth Williams was my interviewee and I ended up bantering with several members of the Carry On Team. I lost control of the interview at one point but had a lot of fun in the process. During the banter I chatted with the Team and proposed a channelled book – Kenneth seemed quite excited about this idea – he is Mr Have-a-Chat that's for sure. His energy is like that of a child with a curiosity about him for the process of being channelled and the possibility of the result being published. He gives a no holds barred discussion about everything – there's no telling where this journey will stop with Kenneth but I did find him perplexing because he would say one thing one minute and then he seemed to contradict himself another – it's probably just semantics at play and interpretation of the words he was sending me, but it was quite a challenge to channel such an amazing intellect.

Alison: Hello, Kenneth, how are you? I can hear you chattering in the background at me.

Kenneth: Well, dear that's because you're easily distracted. I've been around for a few weeks now and watching you deal with life is like watching a hurricane go off.

Alison: Haha thanks a lot for that. It's not that bad is it?

Kenneth: It's not that good! But I do remember what it's like to be human – I liked it when I liked it and hated it when I didn't so you know I can understand you and your hurricane world.

Alison: Well thanks, I think. I can tell you this about my hurricane world: I never thought I'd be getting a ribbing off the strangest talking man on British TV.

Kenneth: Oh my sinuses you're referring to and my extended vowels – all part of the package you know. I talked like that as it got attention. It got people listening to me even if they had no clue what I was saying. I was like that all the time. I used it as a way to get attention shining on me – that's who I was. I can tell you're dying to ask about my sexuality. Well of course I was bent as a nine bob note but not unappreciative of the female form either.

Alison: Thanks for rescuing me on that question as I don't recall it being something very openly discussed about actors before the '80s came and I didn't want to be rude by asking.

Kenneth: Oh my goodness, darling, it wasn't. You'd have your backside up in the air being kicked from here to several eternities down the road if you did – boys were meant to be tough nuts. No pun intended. I couldn't have lived as long as I did if I'd have come clean and everyone knows now of course. I really did appreciate all the sexes, frankly I didn't care – sex was sex to me. I just preferred attachments. (*He means male genitalia.*)

Alison: What about sex itself?

Kenneth: Horrible messy business.

Alison: So not something you enjoyed participating in then?

Kenneth: Well of course I tried it a few times but it wasn't for me.

Alison: So now we've got the sexuality out of the way, what did you enjoy about your life?

Kenneth: Attention, darling, I enjoyed attention. I lived for it. I was made that way – very flamboyant and outgoing and I suppose I just got on with being me – that much I loved. (*This seems at odds with what I've read and heard about him but later on he discusses this more in depth.*)

Alison: Have you any stories you can share about your life – the people you knew and so on?

Kenneth: Barbara and her bra – my favourite scene ever with her boobs let loose on set in Carry On Camping. (*I can't stop laughing the way he talks about it.*) You see that scene wasn't meant to go the way it did. When the delightful Hattie Jacques waded in to take Babs away, she grabbed her arm that pulled her hand away and we got a second flash – it was wonderful. Very hard for me to act my way out of that one I can tell you.

Charles Hawtry: You couldn't act your way out of a paper bag, you cad.

Sid James: Cor blimey those boobs – what a day that was.

Alison: So it looks like you've brought a few friends from your Carry On days with you.

Kenneth: Well that would be right, always bursting in on my scene. They can't help themselves, couple of old hacks – don't improve with age you know. So where were we before they rudely interrupted? Oh yes my interview. So as I was saying, that scene was one of my favourites and as you can see it was everyone's favourite. (*Right now I can see in my mind's eye several of the cast members – I hope they don't all talk at once!*)

Sid: 'Ere we promise to be quiet – much – aha ha ha! Trust Ken to think he was getting all the limelight.

Kenneth: Well I was until you lot of rowdy rabble turned up. Now shush.

Alison: OK. So I'll try to ask questions and see if they can behave but I'm not holding my breath, they seem very mischievous.

Charles: Oh you have no idea, Alison, what we have to put up with.

Alison: I meant you too. [laughter] I'm sure I don't know but it sounds like you're all having a lot of fun.

Charles: There's no other way to be in the afterlife – it's never boring here, always uplifting – it's Carry On Heavenly.

Hattie Jacques: Come now, you boys let Kenneth have his turn before he sulks.

Alison: So, Kenneth, tell me what you think of the afterlife?

Kenneth: Well it's like they say, Carry On Heavenly, it truly is – we're basically all on holidays. Life was so stressful at times you need a holiday to get over it and this is the place to do that.

Alison: OK, so tell me about your philosophies when you were here. Did you believe in Heaven, or God as in a traditional English upbringing?

Kenneth: I was abandoned on a rock, that's how I felt and was brought up strictly religious you know the full English bit but it didn't sit well in my heart because I didn't fit with what it meant to be human in terms of sexuality you see.

Alison: Did you grapple with your sexuality at all or did you just accept it?

Kenneth: I accepted it. I couldn't change my genes and I did feel that I had been stranded on a great big rock for the most part, so I got on with my life as the person that was created here.

Alison: So when you crossed over what did you expect – anything at all?

Kenneth: I expected that if there was an afterlife I would be partying to the very end.

Alison: What about other incarnations? Do you have any of those you'd like to talk about?

Kenneth: I have many incarnations that I could talk about but why talk about them when you can talk about me?

Alison: [laughing] OK so tell me about you then – it's your interview after all – the others have piped down. (*I spoke too soon.*)

Bernard Bresslaw: 'Ere what about me? Why wasn't I invited?

Kenneth: None of you were but you all still managed to find me.

(*I think I've lost control of this interview don't you?*)

Kenneth Connor: Mangy mongrels leaving me out.

Hattie Jacques: Oh stop it, all of you it's like an episode of On the Buses…

Erik Sykes: Rabble, bloody rabble the lot of ya.

All of this banter is in jest. I had to take a rest at this point given the number of actors I could hear. It was very challenging writing out their cross chatter and it was also time to make dinner here. As I was making dinner I was still chatting to them as a group and talking about the possibility of channelling an entire book if they could behave long enough when Charles Hawtrey made an appearance over the others. I had already asked that they give me validations of their presence even though I could see and hear them, it wasn't enough for me because I was having a bit of disbelief: "What? The Carry

On Team wanna talk to me – really?!" in my squeakiest internal voice and so while I was talking to Charles, I got a sharp pain in my left chest cavity that sent shivers down through my bones. It was really unpleasant. I said, "Did you do that?" He replied, "Well you asked for it," and so I did! More proof than I needed but that's Charles!

He died of Peripheral Artery Disease when I looked it up, no doubt giving him a lot of chest pain. I'm grateful he didn't fill me in with his entire symptomology.

After my husband came home and we were eating dinner, Sid James came forward and gave me pain lower down in my chest just beneath the breast bone and not as severe as Charles did thankfully, so I looked up his cause of death. It was a heart attack during performing. He said, "That was from me." I knew it was as I could see him come forward – then Bernard Bresslaw gave me some symptoms. It was pain in my throat and an acidic taste in the mouth and those matched stomach problems so I'm assuming he had some kind of reflux but he also died of a heart attack which he didn't express – of course with so many cast members having heart troubles, it makes sense to express one of his other problems – though without a family member to verify stomach issues I've got no way of knowing for sure other than he said it was him. So our Carry On Heavenly cast of characters was almost complete as I was hoping more of them would come too: hint, hint; Joan Sims, Peter Rogers, Gerald Thomas, Talbot Rothwell, Kenneth Connor, Peter Butterworth, Frankie Howerd and anyone I have forgotten…

Joan Sims: I'm here, love, don't you worry. I'm just sitting back watching the commotion.

This makes my night of course; that the main ones have come to speak in the one interview. This might be a bit of a process to get it all down but I'm ready to channel whatever they want to say.

So my plan of attack for such a project is to let them take over and write their own stories as much as possible with me interjecting occasionally with questions, but basically I'm giving them the floor to talk as much or as little as they like. Kenneth Williams, you first...

Chapter 2: Kenneth Williams

Kenneth: Well I'm delighted of course to be chatting to the real world for a change. I have to put up with this lot over here. I love them dearly of course but you know this constant babble can get downright annoying. (*He's joking.*)

Alison: OK, so tell us anything you want about your life. How you started in film, television, radio, stage – anything. It's your gig now.

Kenneth: I loved the stage. It was wonderfully exhilarating just being up there in front of the audience in all my glory – fresh, live, the thrill was so much more satisfying than the TV or movies because there was room for mistakes and you got instant feedback which of course you could never get with a movie till it was out and then it was too late to fix it.

Alison: Start at the earliest you can remember wanting to be an actor and how you came to be a comedy actor.

Kenneth: Well I was very young. I remember listening to the radio and I was in the army you see so I was able to express myself in the entertainment troop – or corps as some put it. So it went from there. I loved the limelight – that first applause never got old for me – never. And I would meet the most desirable people that gave me guidance – my life as a comedy actor was inevitable. We all had to join the army back then – we were side by side with the Goons, Diana Dors, and oh, Michael Parkinson – he was up and coming in so many ways also. He started as a sports reporter you know but became popular as much like what you're doing now, but clearly the circumstances are quite different. The principle is the same – interviews.

Alison: OK, so go back to your early years of acting and tell us what you did, radio, stage etc. (*I found Kenneth could ramble back and forth and not always coherently.*)

Kenneth: Well I've talked about the stage already and I did do radio as well. I loved it all but radio for me wasn't as instant. It was a delayed audience and nobody got to look at you so it was of course all voice. (*I always thought there was an internal audience?*) Well there was at times.

I made money out of being so camp. Being camp as an actor was quite acceptable but being camp as a real person, it just couldn't be done without ending up broken in a ditch somewhere.

Alison: Can you tell us about your childhood? I mean really speak about the details of growing up? What was it like for you?

Kenneth: I didn't like being a child. I thought it was a complete waste of my time. I wanted to grow up and grow up I did indeed. My father is not a man that I would have wished on anyone else in the world. Of course he's OK now that he's crossed over; that seems to mellow people quite a lot, but as a human being it did not gel with me. He knew deep down that I was not the full quidsin sexually and it didn't sit right with him to have a bisexual but mostly gay son – I hated being in that environment and couldn't grow up fast enough – if it wasn't for conscription I'd have joined anyway just to get away from home.

Alison: Thank you. That's quite a telling paragraph. So can I assume that your relationship was very strained as you were growing up? What was your mother like?

Kenneth: She was like an angel, a beautiful angel. I loved her very much but she wasn't always the healthiest of women but I loved her dearly – her quick wittedness and her propensity to care for others no matter what was happening to her. I was very fortunate with the mother I got.

Alison: OK – so your parents – how much of an influence on your life were they then?

Kenneth: They were very influential. I was made of them and their wild abandon of language and form. My father could cut a person down in one fell swoop with his laser-like tongue and I learned fast and furious how to do the same.

Alison: Your sexuality – I've asked already, was it difficult for you to live with given the way the laws were in England before being gay became a right not a crime?

Kenneth: It plagued me; though I accepted it – it was how I was put together. There's no way about that one can change. You're either gay or you're not. Of course there's levels in between but in my case I was gay but I loved all of it – all things sexy. Deep down I just wanted that contact with another human being. (*Above he said bisexual but mostly gay so I don't know if this is a contradiction or simply for ease of expressions.*)

Alison: What do you mean "that contact"?

Kenneth: Not the physical kind, I wanted male relationships but I also loved women. You can have a sexual desire but not want to have sex. If I wanted sex which mostly I didn't, it would be with a man.

Alison: I see, so you really wanted companionship as much as anything.

Kenneth: Yes I guess that would be right, but how do you find that in a partner where they can live without sex?

Alison: By all accounts you chose abstinence mostly over finding that special someone.

Kenneth: I was inhibited in those days – who wasn't? We could not live openly and I guess even after the laws were taken away that it just stuck – the public just didn't accept that people could be gay so I chose to remain alone and I often thought well, what's the point in all this? But I found my place on the stage that fed me like nothing else ever could. It was like an indelible lover being on the stage; it was my lifeline to feeling something, anything. When I wasn't working I often didn't feel anything at all because I felt wrong – wrongly put in this society abandoned on this great big rock with a sexual composition that was illegal and although there were many who were openly gay in the right rooms of course – they were lonely deep down too. We were always on the lookout for that arresting officer ready to ruin our tête-à-tête so to speak – it was a dodgy business.

Alison: So how did you cope then? Was your entire energy funnelled into working and writing? You were a prolific writer – even down to keeping diaries I understand.

Kenneth: Yes it was the way to express what was inside of me.

Alison: So talk about your work then – how you came to be a comic actor instead of a serious actor.

Kenneth: Well you see I had this face and these eyes and this sound – none of which loaned themselves to seriousness but I could make people laugh and with a nod and a wink and a lot of camp I got a lot of attention, so it was win-win. I did get frustrated with my looks and my voice at times as it just didn't lend itself to serious acting – I couldn't help wanting to make people laugh. I didn't want to be serious deep down.

Alison: Were you suicidal?

Kenneth: All the time I thought about leaving this planet as I struggled to know what I was here for – what was the point, what was it all about? But I didn't go beyond that thought – I know you're wondering did I commit suicide and no I didn't. Though I struggled with depression and darkness in my head I wasn't about to let go of the attention I got from my work. I knew I was here for a reason and perhaps the extensive work and writing that I did was it and if so – then keep doing it no matter what it costs you. (*Kenneth seems to contradict himself quite a bit but he also then verifies at other points what he means. At times it was quite hard to follow where his train of thought was going.*)

Alison: How do you feel about suicide in general then because the community at large thinks you did commit suicide?

Kenneth: It's a way to leave and many people take it – that's their business but it can be premature and I wasn't one of those. I felt that suicide was really a way to give up without really finding your answers – I was stubborn enough to hang around and keep looking for mine.

Alison: You said earlier that you didn't really have any kind of spiritual awakening. Can you expand on that further?

Kenneth: Well of course I was brought up to be the great British Christian but I didn't get the memo – being in the body that I was with the thoughts that I had, I thought well if there is a God he completely beggared up with me – why make something that is illegal? I was illegal. So if that was the truth about God I wasn't interested in it.

Alison: And what about now that you're crossed over?

Kenneth: There is a God – it's everywhere you go here. There's no escaping the feelings that we walk through here or move through I should say. It's very busy but there's always this feeling that you're never alone and it's very comforting and non-judgemental because God doesn't judge and he doesn't make the likes of me as a mistake, we are justified to exist.

(*I found it a little hard to keep up with his thoughts as they rolled from one to another to another with a wild abandonment. It was a challenging effort for me as I felt like I was dealing with an intellect so much higher than mine – brilliant – genius even.*)

Kenneth: About my father – yes – that is a part of my life that I want to talk about – to be honest I think it was a lesson for me to grow up with an extremely homophobic father. He had one idea of what it meant to be a man and that was a misogynistic fartbag who never cried or dared even a whisper in terms of feelings. I absolutely hated him; he was one absolute jackass, to borrow from the American vernacular and it seems fetching to do so. I was an eyesore to him, namby-pamby poo boy with a flair for the ridiculous. He didn't get it how he could have produced such an airy fairy son, yet there I was in all my camp glory, not a muscle on my body, a wiry skinny chap with a pompous how's your father glare. His arse was safe I can tell you that and that's one of the problems with homophobes, they actually think their arses are not safe, but really no self-respecting gay boy wants to go there. Actually, I wasn't sure that I did either even among my peers; I did have a lot of emotional hang ups. I really had no idea what it meant to truly love someone except my mother, that bond was irrefutable for me. I could love that darling woman to the stars and back, but I didn't know how to share my life intimately with a mate. Nothing about relationships or my sexuality made sense to me so I was this misfit with flared nostrils, a wicked stare and an ability to make you and many others laugh.

The day of my death, I was, I admit, having a downer but I wasn't smart enough to work out that combination of drugs was going to kill me so as I've already stated I didn't suicide but it was always there as a potential exit point, that's the reality of it. Mixed up in my head, it wasn't hard to conclude that I was a misfit and only really thrilled when performing. Outside of these performances I was still performing – it never ended. I was always on show – that was the relationship I could have intimacy with. When I was being this person that got attention and made people laugh I felt right at home. I didn't know who the real me was – I'm not as messed up as some other actors you're going to talk to – I know Peter Sellers is thinking of doing this too – he thrived on other personalities, rarely being himself – nice chap.

So anyway, as I was saying, my psychology must've been quite scary while I was in the human body. I was capable of being icy cold – I could cut you to the quick with my laser-like tongue. I was highly intelligent which seems like a contradiction doesn't it? I could've worked that drug combination out if I was going to suicide but I wasn't so I didn't – it just happened and next thing you know I'm standing over my body thinking well that was a disappointing closer. Really I wish I'd died on stage doing what I came to do – entertain people and bring to the fore the complexities of being gay and in the public view. (*This thought seems to come from him as his spirit-self not as his human-self otherwise it contradicts everything he's already said. We have to be mindful of what it means to have a human perspective and spirit's perspective – they are quite different. Once you go home to the afterlife you understand what your life was all about.*) There's no greater exit than to pop off mid-performance and if those around me really knew me they would know suicide just wasn't my style – some did, I know that.

Alison: What was your life like then after you crossed?

Kenneth: It's a strange place what you call the afterlife; we don't exist as you do in a physical way. We're energy and we simply communicate via telepathy – say you could be ten thousand miles away from me but I can send you a thought. I don't need to be right in front of you and we all occupy the same space so to speak. (*This sounds confusing, my interpretation of what he meant is that he's talking about physical miles in distance but that in spirit there is no distance and so communication is instant and I have indeed experienced that many times over.*) Our residence is right here beneath the level of the physical and we can just alter our state to come into your physical awareness. It's a bit like living in jelly, we flux back and forth. There's an air here that belies everything, absolutely everything. It's quite wonderful. I couldn't possibly get depressed because I'm held in the bosom of love and compassion – everywhere is love. It's like bathing in amber nectar; you're just draped in a natural high. People for want of a better word can be anything they want, or travel, either in or out of your 3D space. We have no boundaries, no money worries and we can connect with any individual you can think of and many that you can't. It all depends on you and how advanced you wish to be.

Some people leave the body and live here as if they're still human. There's really no time, nothing is in order and you can access your lives at any point at what you would call time, but time does not exist in the same way for us as it does for you. I spend my time studying and learning and seeking out as much knowledge as I can. I want to expand my awareness up the scales and be in those higher dimensions with the scholars and the masters.

This life I had as Kenneth Williams was a trial for me to understand but eventually, after passing, I was able to gain a great deal of understanding about myself. I am not of any sexual orientation here, as most people here they've left that behind – love is love in all its forms. You don't need to follow the rules of love like earth assumes that there is. There are no rules of love – be with who you want to be with till it no longer suits you to do so. Now if I could've had that as Kenneth Williams I wouldn't have suffered so much. Possibly all the restrictions placed on the proper way to love only served to alienate me from the human race at large – some called me a purist.

My mother, the dear lady, she could make me laugh. She really should've been on the stage herself because she had it all – perhaps that's actually where I got it from in the first place; the yearning to perform. But it was there in me – a calling from a very young age. Of course my father hated that; he wanted to give birth to a bloody bricklayer or some such but I was far too gentle for that. There's no way I was meant for the working class doldrums, as I saw it back then. Truly – I understand I was a right snob – how on earth did that happen? I resented every day in that blasted little pokey house and I couldn't get away from it all fast enough.

When I was in the army the opportunity came up to entertain the troops and my life began to shine like the stars. Dreams come true; I was an actor except I wasn't that good at being serious, had this propensity for making people laugh, satire with my toff impressionism and of course you know the rest but it was then I realised that being abandoned on this rock did have a purpose if I could perform, and I suppose in hindsight that had I been born to another family of class, I'd possibly have missed this opportunity altogether. So there you have it – a star was born and the applause was the reward. It did irk me that I desired to play these serious roles yet my default position is and was thereafter comedy. How could anyone looking and sounding like I did do anything else much to my father's distress? But sod him, I'd grown up and done it my way.

The relationship with my father didn't improve at all. I was everything he didn't want or know how to love and so I was the poster boy for him to hate but what I see now is he thought I was his failure – no matter the successes I had – it was never good enough and I was really over trying to prove myself to him. It took its toll on me and I do believe it affected my ability for intimate commitment. Among the plethora of issues I already faced with society at large.

Alison: I want to ask more about how you felt about acting as so far you've expressed a wild abandonment for it but in your writings you didn't always seem happy with it as your career?

Kenneth: It's not that I wasn't happy with it – I just had a propensity for not liking anything – I was rather messed up in the head. I suppose I probably had some narcissistic disorder that was fulfilled by acting so on one level, I had to like it but it clashed with my disdain for the human race. I had many friends, don't get me wrong. I was able to sustain long term friendships but that next step, I just could not make the leap. I was plagued by notions such as sharing germs. I think the very idea of sharing your private space with another human farting and carrying on was too much. I don't intend to analyse my mind but suffice it to say I probably had a mental disorder to be the way I was. Either that or my IQ was too big and my ego perhaps even bigger. I can look upon my life with a lot of shrewdness now it's been and gone.

Alison: How much of you from this life is still you? Did you absorb it all, take what you needed and so on...?

Kenneth: My personality is shining through as Kenneth Williams. That's for your benefit, but I only kept the good bits. Some might say that's all of it, some say otherwise. I only seek to be what you need so we can communicate my role as a human. I'm not a pompous windbag in the afterlife, though my friends might not agree. (*I feel his wicked playfulness coming across in that statement.*)

Alison: The big question after your own death on everyone's lips still here would be about your father's death – the mystery is how the poison got into the medicine bottle. The police suspected you – are you ready to speak the answer?

Kenneth: (*He sighs deeply and rolls his eyes as if to say oh alright then.*) Well I suppose that question really had to come up but yes I put the poison there. It was mischief gone too far – I never expected him to drink it. I thought he'd smell it wasn't cough medicine and throw it away but the stupid bugger drank it and he got what he deserved and the human race was one bigoted idiot better off.

(I deliberated releasing this part of the channelling because it's so controversial and given that channelling is not perfect if I strongly believe something is true then it can come through as true; I had no such belief so the reader should make their own mind up and given that the media has already reported on this subject, and both Kenneth and Charlie are gone, which they are – then it should not matter that he's giving a posthumous admission. His feelings for his father are not a secret as I understand it but I don't for one minute think that Kenneth wanted to kill his father, I do think it is as he describes further on as a mean prank gone wrong when we revisit the subject.)

Alison: How do you feel about that now?

Kenneth: As Kenneth Williams I don't feel but as a spirit with a much better perspective on the world it probably wasn't the best thing to have done, but Charlie and I have worked out our differences since. I had the capacity to be very cold, icy and frozen. I was cold-hearted to my father, I hated him for hating me; I hated him for being beneath me. I really was quite a snob of the class system but that was my choice and I got what I was looking for. I never forgave my dad, the old bugger, for being such a useless weight around my neck. (*He's very good at changing subjects going from one to another to another with barely a breather in between.*)

Now I've looked at your life and it's been interesting hasn't it, so far and I've spoken to your husband too – the one that's here that is – fascinating fellow, both of you are – some historically significant important bits you've both lived. I'm an old soul too you know but for some reason I came into this life with many hang-ups. [Garbled message] OK, so scrap that. What I'm trying to say is: I could've been the poster boy for hang-ups. My privacy was of the utmost importance to me yet I chose a career that kept me in the limelight so that I had no privacy – perhaps that's another reason I couldn't contemplate intimate relationships. All that body fluid swapping, oh dear, not my cup of tea but I digress – suffice it to say I had my sexual moments but there was no point in time I could share my life with anyone. That's just who I was.

Alison: What did you come here to learn?

Kenneth: Your husband is adorable by the way, such a funny man – he's a delight to hang out with – has this air of sexuality about him that everyone loves to be around.

Alison: You're going to make his head swell and it's big enough already. [laughing] How much did he pay you to tell me that?

Kenneth: Oh you are so awful, darling – no really I mean it, he's a delightful man. I know he had some major control issues when he was there. He's told me that he was very good at getting everyone else to do what he wanted and I'm falling short of manipulative.

Alison: Well yes you've described him well. But he was a master manipulator, getting his own way and people didn't even realise they were being manipulated.

Kenneth: Yes I can see that by some of the things that happened between you. Your mistake was believing that he didn't have an agenda wasn't it?

Alison: (*It's interesting getting marital commentary after the fact by Kenneth. You sort of know he knows everything but doesn't need to say it all.*) Well yes, I guess so but that's a world away now. So let's get back to you and your life or afterlife. What's it truly like living in spirit?

Kenneth: Well it's everything you can dream up and more. There is no right and wrong, no one commits crimes, there are no crimes to commit, there is no judgement except your own judgement. I'm not saying that it's perfect, well I am, but I mean I'm not saying that everyone you meet here is all this love and light stuff – they're not – most are, but some choose to be A-holes. (*He's referring to lower vibrational beings that do not exist in a state of love and happiness and find ways to remain below that vibration when he talks about A-holes.*)

Alison: You mentioned your father has improved since he crossed. Do you spend time with him; have you made friends?

Kenneth: You know that's one story I don't want to tell. He's here, I'm here and that's all there is.

Alison: What about your soul contract with him, did you have one?

Kenneth: Oh well yes, I suppose we did and we both played our roles quite nicely thank you very much, but I'm just not interested in him now. I don't hold any grudges. Like I said, he's here, I'm here, that's all there is. The real story is the story of how we didn't like each other and I've told that story a thousand times.

Alison: Can we readdress the suicide issue? As I understand it you made many references to suicide in your diaries yet you say you wouldn't do that. I don't have access to these diaries but I get that what you wrote then may be different to how you feel now?

Kenneth: Yes these diaries. Now you see if I was going to suicide I might be inclined to destroy my notes about it.

Alison: Really? Why?

Kenneth: Well it's an indictment of my mental health – I mean really I wasn't your average intellect. I could've been a scholar but I chose to entertain people instead. (*I struggled to follow this reasoning somewhat but I thought he was inferring that he was so smart that it messed him up in the head.*)

Alison: So let's lay this suicide issue to rest once and for all – you are definitely saying that you didn't suicide and that it was an accidental overdose?

Kenneth: Yes I am.

Alison: OK thanks, so now can we readdress the issue of your father's death?

Kenneth: Yes that's fine with me as I was so genius as to think he would not be stupid enough to drink poison, then he proved to me that he was by drinking it.

Alison: Is that what you were aiming for – to prove he wasn't or was stupid?

Kenneth: Yes to put it bluntly – I really did not believe he would drink it – that he'd smell it and recoil but the idiot drank it and caused himself a painful passing – not unlike a painful turd. Then he was gone, flushed away from the great big party we call life.

Alison: Do you have any remorse or regrets about his death? (*Bearing in mind that at any point that he refers to his father it is with the utmost venom in his language and his feelings for him.*)

Kenneth: Not at all – I'm not going to hide from anyone or anything in terms of my actions in human form. Look it was wickedness gone wrong, it really was but I don't regret my actions at all.

Alison: That's fair enough I guess. You accept what you did. Tell me what your life review was like?

Kenneth: (*He sighs.*) I liked it when I liked it and hated it when I didn't, just like life itself. It's really an assessment of your own material experience so that if you stuffed up you could see where, when, why and how.

Alison: So in terms of what you came here to do, was it to learn, to teach, or both? You mentioned earlier that you thought your father was a lesson for you.

Kenneth: Yes he was a lesson in tolerance, but I failed miserably. (*He's being ironic.*) What was my life for? That's a jolly good question isn't it? Well I was here to be in the public eye to teach that you could be different to what was normal and still be a wonderful humanoid, though some might not agree with that. (*He smiles a little knowing smile as if to say he knows there are a few that don't.*) Let's just say enough people were affected by my life challenges to discover tolerance and compassion above and beyond what was officially sanctioned to be normal and acceptable.

You know there were many, many, me's in operation; the actor, the thinker, the writer, the troubled soul, the indignant bastard you didn't want to be insulted by – I was a mixed bag of bits really – oh do answer those messages it's very distracting with a ping every five minutes. (*My kids messaging me.*) OK, so where were we? Yes the many, many, me's – it was one superb whirlwind in my head, my thoughts were like the Blackpool Illuminations forever getting switched on and all the different themes in my brain at any given time. It was quite intolerable at times. I was a very fast thinker and the information swirling had to be put somewhere or I might have imploded. You asked me earlier about the posthumous publication of my diaries, well I don't mind that at all, it's one more piece of the Williams' puzzle available for scrutineers. You have already picked up on the speed to which my thoughts can transform into something new but can you imagine living in 3D with that happening in one's brrrain – yes – rouearly. (*I tried to type those two words how he says them there with the extended vowels but it's not easy to replicate in text.*) Don't you love vowels? They are so very round and beautiful sounding. Accents were of great interest but to speak properly with a full vowel sound; that was me – who I was.

Alison: How did your accent develop?

Kenneth: It began quite young. I felt that language was a song to be sung as well as giving one a sense of breeding. I was bred for greater things than pub brawls on a Friday night and I listened, you see, to people with breeding. The radio was a great place to learn how to speak fully rounded and with flair. I thought if that's how these people do it then so will I, and I practiced getting as far away from my working class roots as I could.

Alison: What else can you tell me about living in the afterlife? What does it feel like, touch, taste, smell and so on? What do you see around you? (*No answer as we'd had a break – this sometimes happens, spirits just drop out like losing a call when going under a train tunnel but I could still feel Kenneth around me so I asked if anyone else wanted to answer.*) Who is next then if Kenneth is not chatting...?

Kenneth: Oh I am, dear (*came his rounded reply with a smile and that very wicked sparkle in his eyes*). It's getting to the right moment in the day.

Alison: What does that mean?

Kenneth: I prefer to write at a certain time of the day.

Alison: Ahh OK – so what are we writing about today then now it's time for you?

Kenneth: Well you asked about the afterlife, what our senses experience. It's not like having a nose, eyes, etceterrrra (*rolling the Rs as he does*). You have an all-round experience, no one goes blind here so you can't experience that unless you choose to visualize it briefly. Smells of food or smells in general there isn't any unless you again create them. Here, life is created or as you lot prefer to say manifested out of energy, so if I want to watch a movie I simply access that vibration – ask it to play and I can even manifest my armchair and my flat around it if I choose, or I can download it, (*he didn't specify how this process worked but I suspect he meant think about it and access it via some telepathic experience*), so there's two ways to experience it. A lot of people like to enjoy the old fashioned 3D way and will do what I just said so they can have that experience. You can have whatever you need. You're only restricted by your imagination. There's an endless parade of things to do if you want them exactly like you have but we make them, create them, manifest them in a heartbeat which of course we neither have, then when we're done they go away again. If you wish to be a master golfer or a slalom skiing instructor, then do it, if you wish to be more involved with assisting traffic back and forth to 3D life then do it, we are not restricted one bit. If we want to travel to the furthest regions in space we can do that.

It is so expansive out of the body that one hardly wonders about having one when not in one. That said there are things in physical life we all miss – the sucking on chocolate bars for some is reason enough to come back for. Food is probably one of the most complained about activities that we hear here. (*He's smirking.*)

Alison: So what do you look like to each other and in physical activities such as golf? Is it all a visualization experience or can you become human shaped and create the golf green to play traditional golf?

Kenneth: Oh yes, that's the fun way, create, create, create and do, do, do.

Alison: What do you like to create?

Kenneth: Well I still enjoy my solitude and learning. As previously stated, I love to learn, and I enjoy doing some of that the old fashioned way with a book in my hands in a chair.

Alison: Do you retain that information or does it fade like it does in the human brain if it's not used often?

Kenneth: It's there if you need it and not if you don't. We live on instant life here, there's no need to retain information when you can just access it.

Alison: What do you look like to each other? Do you look like energy or do you look like Kenneth Williams?

Kenneth: Kenneth is only part of my persona, I'm here as Kenneth so you know who I am. We look like what we choose to project but if we so wish, we can float about as energy – in our energetic form. Like stars we glow and sparkle and you've seen souls emanating around people's bodies so you know what I mean. Little tiny spheres of light orbiting.

Alison: Yes that's true I have seen those around people. Does being a spirit blow your mind when you initially cross over or is it like coming back after a long journey?

Kenneth: Well I imagine that it's different for everyone – I mean I got here and went thank God for that. I had

had enough so maybe in some small way those pills were my magic carpet ride out of that life. It was exhausting at the end, always being expected to make people laugh. I felt very tired and was ready for my next challenge so to speak and I had a lot of pain going on that seemed quite unresponsive to medication.

Alison: Do you feel you achieved everything you came here to do or would you change your life in any way?

Kenneth: No I wouldn't change a thing. I own the life I was in and in many ways it gave me so much to live for – without my acting, now that would be a different story – imagine me and a pair of overalls going – how's your father, missus? Need a new paint job? I'd be run out of town. I fit where I was – but as misfits go I fit that too in myself.

Alison: How much contact with the cast of Carry On, do you have now?

Kenneth: Well as you can see where there's a chance at the limelight, Charles will be first to wade in. He's being ever so patient over here but in terms of seeing each other, we do catch-up and all these little foibles that we like or didn't like about each other are really not an issue. (*He's giving me the impression he's talking about Sid James here so I assume they didn't always get along.*) Sid was not always someone I saw eye to eye with so yes, that's who I meant.

Chapter 3: Joan Sims and the Team

Sid: You got that right. Cor blimey aha ha ha ha. At least I wasn't bloody unbearable like Charles could be. (*He winks at me.*)

Charles: Speak for *yourself, I say.* (*He feigns an indignant air but it's in fun.*)

Sid: Mind you, with Kenny hogging the limelight it's a wonder any of us got along. Lucky me I had a laugh that could drop knickers.

Alison: (*I burst out laughing...*) Again it went quiet so I asked if anyone else was stepping in.

Kenneth: I'm not finished, just letting the rabble off their chain before they chew my arm off first for chatting this long.

Hattie: Imagine, dear, this going on. On set at every turn there was someone ribbing someone for something. All fun and games. (*She's such a beautiful lady.*)

Joan: They were like a bunch of peacocks half the time and with Kenneth farting it was all very exhausting.

Bernard: I was the gentle giant.

Joan: You were not as I recall it. I remember you singing – oh dear oh dear. But I loved you in pantomime. Played wonderful roles there. I miss the Christmas periods with the dark nights and the crisp winter air before the shows come on to an audience of smiling kids.

Alison: What else do you miss, Joan?

Joan: I miss it all; my life was filled with so many happy memories. Of course like everyone has, there were dark periods where I shrunk into a slump, but I got myself up and out of it.

Alison: What do you think inspired you to become an actress in the first place?

Joan: As you know I was brought up on Langdon Station and I got lots of attention performing for the customers. I played dress ups, and created character roles for myself. The passengers loved it much to my father's disgust but nothing he said or did could dissuade me from this path. I simply loved to perform, couldn't help it. It's a theme you'll find running through all of us that we loved the attention given to us by an audience. You know some people think that all actors are troubled in some way and perhaps they are. We all have our lonely moments.

Alison: Do you regret anything about your life here?

Joan: Not as much now we've left it behind. I really rarely think of it in terms of any sort of regret because look at how wonderful my career was and the people I got to spend time with. When you're sitting side by side with a person and you can't stop laughing for no reason and getting paid to do it you have to love that, and I did.

Alison: Was comedy always going to be your forte?

Joan: Oh I think so yes – happy face – that was me. I lit up when I was on stage and it was almost impossible for me to be anything but comical. I had my serious moments early on but the direction I went in was clear – comedy acting.

Alison: What about your love life? That didn't seem to run as smoothly as your career.

Joan: And this is why I say people think performers or artists of any kind really, are troubled, but you don't have to be artistic to be troubled and have a lousy love life. I was lonely when I was away from performing. I was a loyal child to my parents and it just didn't sit right having relationships with men as if it was character destroying for them. So although I had my lovers I always felt compelled to be what they wanted – a sort of untouched doll that gets taken off the shelf once in a while for a dusting and then put back.

Alison: This sounds really sad – was it loyalty, I mean or were you worried about them feeling embarrassed about you doing something they didn't approve of?

Joan: I suppose yes that could be it, whereas in the movies and on stage it was a profession and although the Carry On was cheeky it was still respectable.

Alison: What is respectable though in this context?

Kenneth: Respectable was not being gay. (*He laughed – I've started calling him Kenny as it seems I feel I know him quite well now. He says the word respectable in that emphasised way, fully rounded.*)

Kenneth: Respectable was not having torrid affairs, respectable was not being drunk and disorderly in the streets, respectable was no sex I'm British. All life with the fun stuff left out you see and when you had compassion, love and respect for yourself and your family you had to worry all the time about what they thought. It was a nightmare. The number of people who hold themselves back to be respectable and end up on the bottle because they repress hopes and dreams is outrageous you know.

Joan: I should know about that, it was a problem for me for many years and when I lost you [Kenny] and Hattie I was very lonely. We were all misfits together, you [Hattie and Kenny] were my family that I could be myself with and not worry about respectability – I didn't go to Hattie's funeral. It was an awful day. Couldn't bear to say goodbye, but I didn't realise it wasn't goodbye, it was see you later and now here we all are – Carrying On Heavenly – oh I do like that title. (*She gives a little cheeky laugh.*)

Bernard: She missed me the most. (*I don't know if that's true but I'm definitely picking up some beautiful and genuine appreciation between Bernard and Joan. It's a very genuine affection for each other.*)

Joan: Our lives were gruelling on the Carry On show because of the long hours sometimes. Well more often than not the weather was appalling. We'd try to pretend it was a hot day in our bikinis but we were frozen, blue lips and nipples everywhere. But I wouldn't trade a thing about it – more pay would've been nice. We didn't get very much for the work we did back then. Not like the American counterparts were getting paid or the men for that matter, but again, I'm looking back through hindsight. The truth is, I loved my job. It made me feel like I belonged to something great and no matter what the conditions, it's a ride I wouldn't change for any reason: and just look at the relationships that evolved from it. We learned unconditionally to love each other if we didn't always know it at the time.

Alison: I spoke briefly to Frankie Howerd a few months ago, I'm hoping he joins us too as I know you and he got on well. (*I knew Frankie was around but he doesn't say much – in character I often hear him with his familiar "Ooo I say" as if all the world is gossip to be surprised by.*)

Frankie: Well, you know, Joan and I, we couldn't stop laughing; it was one big giggle after another. I only had to look at her and she set off.

Joan: Oh yes, we did so resonate together didn't we? Shall we tell them why?

Frankie: Oh go on then.

Joan: Vibrations – we vibrated at a frequency that created laughter between us.

Frankie: The world will think you're mad telling them that, Joan.

Joan: We didn't know why when we were there but we do now. (*I can see them chatting to each other in my third eye and walking off but I can no longer hear this conversation.*)

Kenneth: Look at them, so easily distracted. But as Joan said the job wasn't perfect. It had more problems while performing it than not but you can't take away that experience from the friendships and that the end result made people laugh in droves. You might call us comedy light workers. The perception is as stated that entertainers are troubled but perhaps we were supposed to be so we could perform and make people happy.

Alison: Do you think that's a theme among comedy performers, to help keep people happy?

Kenneth: I do, yes, of course and because we're in the public eye we also bring to the fore issues that may have been suppressed like sexuality you see. There's so much more going on in the world than war and hate – there has to be a balance struck. Well that's the job of the creative arts and artists. We lift people up and out of the heaviness we call life.

Alison: That makes a lot of sense to me.

Joan: The creative arts are a passive way to enlighten people about subjects that might otherwise be taboo. Robin Williams' comedy genius among others did it so eloquently and in doing so also taught not to take life so seriously. So our doom and gloom personal lives, our foibles and all that get a public airing which helps others with the same problems not feel so isolated and we address concerns, issues and problems in a less fierce way. We really are all the geniuses in this regard – laughter is the best teacher. Comedy light worker is a good descriptor for what comedy is beneath the laughter.

Alison: So is that in the soul contract of all artists then as it seems obvious now you've both touched on it?

Joan: It is in every soul contract where a person is in the public eye to give some type of performance or artistic talent, that they are to affect the public in a certain way and not always is it a fun, laughter, comedy way. The visual arts highlight all ideas of things that are current affairs. (*She's putting the painting "The Scream" in my head as an example of what she's talking about.*) So you see that type of art elicits quite a different response and the audience is not laughing but is confronted by an emotional image that they carry with them for the rest of their lives. So there are many types of effectual soul contracts and without touching on the obvious too much, look at what Hitler did and how during that time entertainers were brought in to raise the troop morale. It's all about balance, there must be an outlet for the greater good in all things or a miserable world it would be. Earth and humans need a balancer to keep it from swinging fully into darkness.

Alison: This is so interesting, thank you for that information.

Joan: You're welcome, dear – go have a rest and we'll talk again later. (*So rest I did. Channelling so many spirits at once drains me.*)

Alison: Hello again. I can feel you around me. Are you ready to go again?

Kenny: We are indeed. What a busy few days it's been for you. We're enjoying your book as you read it. Hope it goes well. (*He's meaning my fantasy books I was editing at the time for publication.*)

Alison: Thanks, Kenny.

Kenny: I'm not one for dragons normally but you do portray them well and they are such magnificent creatures.

Alison: Thank you. What shall we talk about today then?

Kenny: Well I've been chatting to your dad. He's a good chap and working very hard to support you. He's learning all sorts about his spiritual self, much of which he would've forgotten. We all get that when we cross back over here. Some don't bother to find out who they are and pick up where they left off on their human journey. Your dad's not one of them – he's really getting stuck into knowledge. You should be proud. (*Kenneth smiled widely and gave me what seemed like an elbow nudge. I'll try to describe this as it happens: as I'm sitting communicating, my physical eyes know where a spirit is in proximity to my location. Sometimes I see them clearly, other times that information is then processed by my third eye which is like looking through a tunnel most of the time, it's often grainy and shadowy, and the other information is given as a knowing that he was giving me the elbow nudge.*)

Alison: I am very much so.

Kenny: I do so wish my relationship could've been more like yours – oh yes I know he was a bit of a Victorian but he never rejected you did he? (*I'm getting a knowing look from Kenny, it's making me smile. Kenny is a very knowledgeable spirit. He's learning as much about me as I am about him.)*

Hattie: He's just nosey, dear. (*She jokes – Kenny winks.*)

Joan: He'll be your best friend by the time we're done and that's in the nicest way – he's a wonderful old soul is our Kenny.

Alison: Thanks, Joan. Tell me, how was your life review after you crossed?

Joan: (*She's thinking.*) It's hard to say really, I was foggy brained by all this when I crossed – a bit like one of your kangaroos in the headlights. (*She laughs.*) It was sixes and sevens for me I suppose you'd call it. I think I held myself back in life if I'm honest as much as that probably sounds crazy from your point of view. I really was restrained and that came through in my life review on several occasions. I still wouldn't change a thing about it.

Alison: What were you here to learn and teach?

Joan: That's easy. I was here to learn to laugh and laugh I did but not always. I didn't do so good on the love front but that's not to say I wasn't loved, I know I was, very much so. But I'm talking about romantic love. I held myself back there and could've done better.

Alison: Does that even matter when you had many other types of successful relationships?

Joan: Oh no, of course not, dear. We are not perfect beings, we are here to learn about love in all its varieties.

Alison: What about other lives – are there any that you felt related to this life?

Joan: Well I was an African tribeswoman, (*she's showing me a beautiful image of a tall African woman with metal rings around her neck*) and I guess you could compare that one tribe to the Carry On tribe. I mean we all needed each other to function. We were family so my life in Africa was much the same in that regard. We supported each other, each playing our role within that community and we protected each other. It was before Westerners came to Africa so it was a very traditional life and as women we were equal in our duties even if to some that seems unequal. Being the women of the tribe, we were the nurturers. The boys of Carry On needed nurturing. Ahahahah. (*She lets out a very cheeky high pitched laugh.*)

Alison: (*Frankie Howard appears in my third eye as I'd stopped talking to Joan to do some exercise and have a break.*) Hello, Frankie. Did you want to chat or are you just hanging out with your friends?

Frankie: Well watching you exercise is making me glad I'm no longer human. I'm all puffed out just watching.

Alison: You've been popping in and out on me for some time now though, so just to say hi or did you want to be part of this project?

Frankie: I don't like being part of any projects these days you know. I'm all for kicking back and relaxing – none of that communication nonsense. No I'm just here to support you on your journey and little things like that. You've got a good soul and life's not been easy for you, love. So why not lend support? That's what I'm doing; besides I'm having a laugh with your dad. He's quite a character when he gets going. Our age group you know – he understands us – yes he's been getting around and that nice chap Erik – we like him. (*He's talking about Erik Medhus from the Channelling Erik blog.*)

Alison: Oh wonderful. Sounds like a lot of fun over there.

Frankie: Ay, now don't go getting ideas that being here is better than being there.

Alison: [Laughing] OK I won't. (*He waves a finger at me and peers over his glasses.*)

Frankie: It is, but learning stuff there – that's not the same you know, not the same. (*In his company I always feel like we're a couple of old girls having a bit of a gossip, hehe.*)

Alison: It's hard not to wonder the difference when it all sounds so lovely after crossing over, like a great big holiday.

Frankie: Well it is, my girl, but you have to earn it first – holidays – work then play – plenty more for you down there happening. You mark my words, it's all about to explode for you so enjoy that when it comes.

Alison: Thanks, not sure what you're getting at but I'll take it on board as something to ponder.

Frankie: Right I'm off now – behave – as if you will – your dad and me are off for a pint – cheerio.

Dad: I never thought about any of this, our Ali, when I had a body. Thanks to you though I'm meeting lots of people I never thought I could meet. It's very enjoyable this afterlife stuff and I'm glad my daughter is so open to it and I can talk to you anytime I want to.

Alison: Thanks, Dad. Off you go for your pint with Frankie. Love you.

Dad: Aye, love you too.

Chapter 4: Bernard Bresslaw

Alison: *I never know what's coming next with this Carry On lot but I always know when it's time to chat 'cause they start to talk about my day and what I've been doing – it's really such a good life to have these spirits in it – it comforts me that the world we're living in really is just a school house, or an adlib play that we will eventually exit and that they're hanging out with my dad and Erik Medhus – it couldn't get any better to know these things. Bernard Bresslaw came forward stating he was ready. What a lovely man he is; very soft in nature, his energy is just lovely.*

Bernard: I'm ready for a chat.

Alison: How did you get started in acting then and Joan mentioned earlier about your singing? I didn't know you were a singer.

Bernard: She laughs, but I had a nice voice, just not the look to go with it ya see? It wasn't meant to be my singing career but in them days and I'm talking about before you were born we had to be all-rounders, do a bit of everyfink. You couldn't really specialise, as an audience had big expectations. They were going to get a bit of dance hall, a bit of a larf and a lot of bang for their money. We were all brought up to that type of entertainment so yeah I had a few singles aht along the way, but it wasn't a long term career goal. (*His accent starts to come through in this channelling – sometimes they will ramp up things like that if I'm asking doubtful questions in my head about who I'm talking to.*) I liked singing, don't get me wrong, was always doing it much to Joan's surprise – she won't admit it but she laved it [jokingly]. I was a big jolly giant, I was the dorky one – you'll notice not one of us had a serious face on – most of us had rubbery faces so they were funny. Sent there to entertain that was our lot in life. We all laved what we did, ya know?

Alison: Yeah, it certainly looks and sounds like you did. What was your spiritual mission here was it to learn, or teach, or both?

Bernard: I never learned anyfink in terms of academic stuff, that was Kenny, but I did learn to love myself, big dorky bloke, big heart, that was me.

Alison: So how and when did you know you were going to entertain people?

Bernard: Dance hall days; that was everyfink when I was younger. I love dance halls, like singing, lots of couples moving around the dance floor – very much a family environment. We were close as people then, we had a care for each other.

Alison: Sounds sentimental.

Bernard: I am being sentimental in a way. (*I'm having trouble getting Bernard to focus on the questions about his career. He's telling his own story.*)

Kenny W: Mmmm yes we can see that Bernard is not focused.

Alison: Just talk about what you'd like to talk about, Bernard then if my questions aren't hitting the mark.

Bernard: I'm reminiscing. I've not thought about this life for quite some time in any depth. It was a good life; I enjoyed it. Always seemed to land on me feet with acting in one form or another.

Alison: OK, so what about the afterlife then, how is that for you?

Bernard: I like it, it's peaceful here and you can do what you want – you're not restricted and there's a lot of love. Music everywhere, like being in a wonderland; it can mesmerise you if you let it. Imagine ancient Greece with meditation and no class system. It's really perfect.

Alison: What do you like to do there? (*It struck me after hearing him talk about not thinking about the life as Bernard for some time that why would he need to? Why would any of us need to once it's done unless you still had things to do here? Once the spirit has returned to the afterlife dimensions then they integrate back into the highest self as I understand it, and the attributes of the person become part of many other attributes of the over-soul: meaning that for Bernard to come here and chat as Bernard, he has to revisit that exact person that he was in this life that we know him in, and that might take some time to find among everything else they do as a soul.*)

Bernard: Read books, I like to read a lot and absorb lots of information. Catch up with family and these lot are always a larf. We're still quite close and it's not just the Carry On Team we keep in touch with, there's the gang from The Army Game and all our other haunts. It's like a repository for British comedy stars round 'ere at the moment – you keep seeing Dick Emery for a reason back there – he's waiting for an interview and Max Bygraves, he's another. You're going to be very busy – your chosen career is going to be filled with these spirits now the word's aht. (*He laughs.*)

Alison: I did wonder about Dick Emery being around. So let's keep talking about you though.

Bernard: Right, well my career was the highlight of my life. It really flowed after NIDA. I just couldn't do wrong and when Carry On came along it was even better, but conditions were very harsh. It was gruelling work, worth it for the reward it gave all of us though. I guess you could say I was the lesser troubled team member. I was happy for the most part, so not much controversy. The life plan worked aht for me, apart from the singing that is – I know you don't think I had a voice of an angel after finding my old tunes online – I've no idea why. (*I just realised he's joking about his singing voice, it's very subtle. The first time he mentioned he had a nice voice I didn't realise it was a joke. He's one of those jokers that keeps a straight face to make you believe a story then laughs when you believe it.*)

Bernard: You've blown my MO right aht of the water there. (*I giggled.*) So as a 6 foot 7 inch giant I was always being asked to get things off high shelves – you should've seen the camera crew trying to work out shots with all the shorties in them with me – what a larf that was. You're dying to ask about the panto you saw me in aren't you?

Alison: Hehe yes.

Bernard: Long time ago for you and you can't remember where it was?

Alison: No I can't. I just remember being in awe of seeing you on stage and knowing you were a movie star.

Bernard: Manchester, it was in the '70s, you were a kid – you loved panto. I didn't see you in the audience (*he's joking again*) but I knew you were there. (*Still joking.*)

Alison: I came home thrilled that I'd seen you on stage. I loved Carry On movies – they were very naughty and cheeky and funny. You all fascinated me on screen.

Bernard: You were curious about the people behind the roles, even back then you were wanting to know what made people tick weren't you? (*Who's interviewing who here? Haha.*) You're a lovely old soul, Alison.

Alison: Aww shucks, thank you, that's very nice of you to say but tell me more about you. (*Feeling a little under the spotlight there.*) What can you tell us about your life review – how did that experience go?

Bernard: When you make people larf for a career, life reviews tickle 'cause you get to experience the full force of that from the people's point of view. My review was wonderful in that regard. I've had other life reviews not so fun though. But I did enjoy this one.

Alison: So you succeeded in the life you had as Bernie – no complaints?

Bernard: Only about the size of my feet – do you know how hard it is to buy shoes when your feet are big enough to hold this stature up?

Alison: (*I burst out laughing again.*) How big were they?

Bernard: Size 12 I think.

Sid: Cor blimey, like strapping barges to your feet – wanna try falling over them on set – Bernie was quite a size to orient around.

Charles: Not 'alf – but the most loveable of a giant.

Alison: He is sweet natured that's for sure. I want to call him Uncle Bernie. So what else did life reveal for you when you watched the review, Bernard?

Bernard: Love – love conquers all and in making people larf I gave a lot of love to the people of Britain and that's all you can ask of yourself in the life you lead – love. How much of it did you give, how much of it did you generate around and inside you? If you led anything else but a life of love then that's not why you're here, love it, give it, create it.

Alison: So what about people who suffer badly in their lives from emotional trouble?

Bernard: Victims – victims need to learn to love themselves and that goes for their criminal abusers, love is the right path. Non-judgement is pure love.

Alison: Were you a religious man then?

Bernard: Not in the sense of religion but I had my ideas about what was to come after my life had ended. I was brought up with Christian-values (*I read he was from a Jewish family so I assume he meant Christian-Judeo but never asked further about this*) just like the majority of Britain was back then but something didn't ring true for me. I felt that love was not a fear monger and religions were fear-based not love-based. It's a contradiction to say love the Lord or else, that's judgement and we only judge ourselves. God isn't some maniacal thief that steals your eternity away because of his own ego. He would never do that and he's not a he. There's not a word to describe him except pure love – there's the freewill ability to do with your individualism what you want to; God can learn from you as himself. We're made of the same stuff. It would be like putting yourself in jail for disagreeing with yourself – nah, that's just daft. You create your own reality so if you believe in hell you may create a reality where you go there but it doesn't exist unless you create it so don't create it – those that do struggle to transition half the time because they fear hell – it's not real. The only thing that's real is there's an afterlife and we all go to it when we die, so set your beliefs up to it and your transition will be easy.

Alison: Can you tell us more about the God source? What do you call it where you are?

Bernard: Love source I call it, love source 'cause that's what it generates and we all know that we are made of it and that we've been given our individuality as a form of artistic expression of that love source.

Alison: God is an artist – a great director casting for a random system of practical learning then?

Bernard: That's right and quite a profound way to describe love source. Its intelligence goes beyond anything you can even imagine and its vastness radiates out to regions of space you didn't know existed and the levels of its vibration, like many stacks of plates, all exist in one space overlapping and functioning in unity. That people of earth are being told that God is a separate being commanding worship is a right load of old tosh. That's fear, that's human beliefs created from their egos. It's time that thought was broken so that the answer to why you're all here is love, one step at a time.

Alison: Ahh this is getting really deep now. So can you tell me about your thoughts on the world as it is today?

Bernard: It needs a love bomb to go orf under it. I don't want to get into politics but there's a lot of manoeuvring abaht to keep the vibration low on earth, but IT'S FAILING. The vibration's been lifting for years and years as more people wake up to the truth that we are all one source and that is love source.

Alison: OK and awesome too. Can we shift gears back to you again now and what you were here to learn, or to teach, or both?

Bernard: Laughter and love – to give the best you could give at all times and I think I achieved it for the most part. I wasn't here to teach it to anyone but myself but in doing that I hope it had a teaching effect.

Alison: You've turned out to be quite a surprise to interview. You're very intelligent spiritually.

Bernard: I'm an old soul too. We all are, though some of us wonder about Charles' mission. (*Joking.*)

Chapter 5: Bernard the Love Guru

Charles: Oi! I can hear you. (*Pretends to be indignant.*) My life was a challenge because I was a lonely gay man in a society known for its persecution of gay men – that meant finding love was fraught with combat. It was a fight to be gay. We were ostracised for it, oh the world loved a gay man in comedy; they're funny when they're camp but the actual nuances of being gay in the flesh were a nightmare and I was desperately lonely. I loved my job entertaining, it lifted me somewhat, but as I got older I mushed my brain with booze and tried flushing the loneliness away in a drunken stupor to the point where I was never sober. I was glad to leave my body behind and cross over myself. Being human this time round was quite an ordeal for me.

Alison: I'm sorry to hear that, Charles. What was your spiritual contract here then?

Charles: Living a life of being a gay in the movies so everyone who wasn't gay could see gay people need love too and were not freaks, were real, were actually the antipathy of love because we are capable of loving men. Those of us who love men have loved women in other lives and to do it in this life is not necessarily out of our agenda, but we are in search of love. I didn't connect to myself at all; I was lost and incapable of self-love. I really loathed myself because I didn't understand myself. It was a conflict to be gay when the church said we were evil incarnate then that hit at our core self-esteem. We weren't evil, there's no evil, there is only love and various types of it to learn about. I didn't learn well enough that lesson in the body but I understand it well enough now. I've still got a lot more to learn but I've no intentions of being human again for some time.

Alison: You sound very unhappy about your life, was there a time when you were happy?

Charles: Acting, when I was acting and even that lost its lustre in the end. I couldn't function because of my booze problem and no one wanted me on set. I was unreliable and drunk when I did show up for work.

Bernard: It wasn't easy for any gay man to deal with their feelings. Things have come a long way since then – counselling was almost out of the question – who could you trust when your very fibre, every part of you was illegal?

Alison: You have a good understanding of what it was probably like for gay people, Bernard.

Bernard: Not surprising. I worked wiv three of 'em or more and they suffered terribly yet all were good men. I could see their conflicts within themselves. I always felt quite helpless for them; life was hard enough without throwing in the gay baton so to speak. You gotta admire a person who chooses to come here and bring these things out in the open. They are unsung heroes. (*He's a really emotionally advanced soul.*)

Alison: What about your marriage to Betty – still together now?

Bernard: She's the love of my life even to this day. She is with me and has been with me on many a life. We're a soul grouping. We enjoy each other's company a great deal and I wouldn't have it any other way. As long as Betty is happy, I'm happy. We had our moments but things were different then – the structure of marriage worked as long as there was respect for each other and I know you're wondering about the whole patriarchal thing but it didn't have to be like that either. Respect for each other to function in certain roles didn't mean a wife couldn't explore her own dreams. Only marriages where respect and equality doesn't exist, fail. Our marriage worked because of that. I loved my wife no matter what else she chose to do. Modern marriages often compete between the couples and often have no respect – there's a lot of selfishness out there – there probably always has been – I'm not sure where I'm going with this. (*I burst out laughing 'cause it sounded like Bernie was really letting his mind wander then he realised he was waffling.*)

Alison: I get it, though, what you mean. Respect for each other is a good foundation for a marriage.

Bernard: Yes, that's what I was getting at in a tongue-tied way. (*He's such a sweetheart.*) Comes back to love – when there's love there's no ego. Ego has a lot to answer for in human relationships. Ego is always competing for first place and that's out of insecurity in my book. Then there's conflicting teachings which set children on a path of heads down bums up don't get above your station – it's no wonder so many people have ego problems. No, what the human race needs to know is that every single one of them is equal and there's no class above or below; all one. (*Basically what he's saying is that our teachings mess us up from a very early age – there is always exclusivity which creates ego problems when a person is treated differently, for example. At least that's how I understood his feelings as he was talking.*)

Alison: (*Had a day's break.*) Who's on today then for a chat? (*This was 04/08/2015.*)

Bernard: I wanna talk about meditation and how there's not enough of it going on. There's a block that it belongs to the enlightened ones but it belongs to everyone and there's nothing to fear. I know from observation that people give it two minutes then think about doing the washing and give up. The trick is to let the thought pass and the next one till eventually all the worries and woes have filtered through the brain and the brain settles down. It takes practise and the more people do it the easier it will come. It's like any skill – you can't drive a car the minute you get behind the wheel [first time] so why should meditation be any different? (*While he's talking to me he's also chatting to Joan. I can hear their voices but not the words.*) People give up too easy – that's all it is because they can't see the benefit of it but the benefits would include making them better drivers that's for sure. (*I love that logic, and he's teaching through humour.*)

Alison: You've given me a lot of spiritual information I wasn't expecting, Bernard. Is this an area you are passionate about?

Bernard: I work in this area. I try to get through to people about love, the vibration of love and what it can do to help people. So much anger in the world that doesn't need to exist, it really doesn't, so I like to channel this message to people – help them if I can.

Kenny: He's quite the Zen master isn't he?

Alison: Yes he is and it's a surprise to learn about it.

Kenny: We all support him in this endeavour. Sending love out to the masses. He's really a blessing in disguise.

Alison: I can see that. Are there many spirits doing this type of work?

Bernard: Yes there are and the numbers are growing in masses as things are shifting to make the transitions that are coming a softer landing for everyone.

Chapter 6: Sid James

Alison: (*I took a couple of days' break for a few other projects and readings then when I came back Sid was ready to talk.*) Hey, Sid. Thanks for coming to chat. You were with me when I watched the Carry On Darkly doco about you last night and were worried my opinion changed because of what I learned. It hasn't, I get that people are a certain way in the body that can't adequately be explained till after death has occurred, but now you're in the afterlife, tell me about the way you were with women and so on.

Sid: I want you to know that I have the utmost respect for women but wasn't very good at containing my anger in life. I had to have my own way more often than not – believe me, I would've punched a bloke just as easily. I was hot headed but I loved women, I wanted it all not realising what I had was good enough. I didn't understand love on the deepest levels, I became frustrated quickly but there's more to me than what you saw.

Alison: I know there is, you don't have to worry about that. You're showing me images of Barbara Windsor.

Sid: Love of my life that woman. I didn't know what love was till I met Barbara. She lit up the room with her personality, her cheeky saucy nature. She had me in every way emotionally possible, hook, line and sinker and I didn't understand that to love was to be understanding, instead I was possessive. I know now that came from my own insecurities. I was insecure, I mean look at me, face like a bashed prune, who would want Sidney James if not for the laughter, the jokes, the laugh, the cheek?

The package outside of the looks is what I had and I felt deeply insecure that some big, hulking, good looking brute, which basically was anyone else but me, would sweep her away so I stifled her and you can't do that to a magnificent butterfly without killing the roses she lands on so that was my lesson in life – there's more to love than ownership. Love is not about looks, it's about understanding one's self, loving one's self no matter what the packaging and I was a player all my life. I was much better looking in my youth mind you.

Alison: You're showing me images of your days as a hairdresser now. Why is that?

Sid: That's when I was much prettier.

Alison: Why did you invent a life history instead of telling the truth about your pre-acting days?

Sid: Better story wannit? Better than a hairdresser I thought, wanted some glamour thrown in for good measure. I thought if people knew I was a hairdresser they'd think I was a nancy-boy and wanna box me anyway – all ego ya see. Mine was fragile and I had an addictive personality to go with it. My girl Hattie made all the difference. I'd probably have gone dahn the tube much faster had it not been for the sensible voice of Hattie. She was and still is a dear friend. She had her own inner demons but always seemed to act as the voice of reason for the rest of us misfits. We are a soul family.

Alison: What about acting itself then how did you find yourself attracted to that?

Sid: It was glamour and money but not much bloody money in them Carry On movies; had to work our own schemes for that to work. We were experts at product placement before the term was even invented – flamin' had to be with the tight bastards running the show, cor blimey. All we wanted was a lifestyle ya know, to go with the hard graft we all put aht and believe you me – we all flamin' grafted, cor blimey. Dawn till flamin' dusk most days on set. It was a bloody marathon from start to finish cutting those movies. I'm deserving and enjoying of this life I've got 'ere now.

Alison: I'll bet you are too, it sounds lovely. I expect the women you romanced, most of them are crossed over, have they forgiven you for being a player?

Sid: Well if they 'aven't it's their problem 'cause it's all good here in that respect, forgive and forget, well not forget but you know what I mean. You can't carry that stuff on, it's too hard – this place is like a love museum, it's flamin' everywhere – very hard to not forgive and those that manage it often don't vibrate up this high, they stay down low towards 3D levels – plenty of that down there.

Alison: So do you have any regrets?

Sid: Yeah my behaviour with women. Lessons learned – love is abaht understanding each other and not possessing each other. It's abaht doing the right thing and letting each other blossom and grow. I didn't get it then but now I do. Lesson learned.

Alison: What about the gambling addictions?

Sid: Taught me I wasn't happy in the moment and always wanting more, more, more.

Alison: What was your life review like?

Sid: Cor blimey, I was waiting for that one. Basically it was both a slap in the face and also very pleasant 'cause I made a lot of people larf. That was what I was meant to do and I did it well. Aha ha ha ha. (*He's still got that dirty laugh.*)

Alison: Any plans to come back?

Sid: Not in any flamin' hurry that's for sure. I'm enjoying this lifestyle here. I don't need money and there's plenty of love. I can create what I want. (*He's showing me horseracing.*) I still enjoy that type of thing but there's no guilt associated with it on this side of the veil.

Alison: Is there guilt associated with gambling on the 3D side do you think?

Sid: Plenty, we know it's not good for us because it takes us away from reality and making it better. (*This is from the point of view of a gambling addiction.*) We throw ourselves into these situations that mask the pain – pain of being unhappy with ourselves. We think that gambling will change everything when we win big but we never win big, so when we lose – reality is still there and guilt for spending the money as well.

Alison: That must create a lot of inner conflict?

Sid: You betcha it did – and anger which you took aht on the people you loved. Val was my saving grace but I didn't look after her properly. I didn't know what an angel she really was. She has forgiven me, I know that.

Alison: That's good then. What advice would you give to people with gambling problems?

Sid: Gotta look inside and find out why, what's causing it. Looks ain't everything you see. I proved that by a sparkle in my eye and a good sense of humour, but it was always a conquest to lift me up. It was selfish of me, I squandered women like money. Look inside, find what's missing, find your heart, connect to it and just be love.

Alison: What do you miss about being here the most?

Sid: The highs and lows. We tend to live at one level all the time here, there's no rollercoaster ride of emotions. It's always fun and sometimes I wonder abaht feeling contemplative, not that I am by nature but there's feelings you access in a 3D environment that are almost impossible to hit on here so I miss that, and a good cigar and whiskey. It's not that we can't have those things but there's a world of difference; feeling the ritual of a smoke and a drink is what we do here. We imagine it and it's in front of us but there's no friction as that drink goes down. It's missing its solid touch; that's abaht it for me.

Alison: Have you had other lives you'd like to share with us?

Sid: I've had several lives in South Africa. I've been a great white hunter which I know is frowned upon now but it wasn't then. It's like anything; we have to start enjoying the world as part of it, not trying to conquer it. I moved around a lot in that life too, back when the locals had no choice to respect the white fella.

Alison: Did that life influence this one?

Sid: In a way I was trying to conquer in both lives instead of learning to live from within. I've got a long way to go but I've also learned a lot and when I have another life I will be better off for it. I'm not talking abaht time here, I can hear you wondering – no point trying to put it into those terms, time is meaningless. (*Haha there's no escaping your own thoughts in these interviews.*)

Alison: Ah huh, OK yeah – I can also hear yours and your personality is coming across.

Sid: Give us a kiss.

Alison: Yeah! That's what I heard. [Laughing]

Sid: Make ya larf ya see. (*He's got that cheeky grin and sparkle in his eyes.*)

Alison: It did – that's the Sid I know from TV. Did you have anything else to add to these questions? What about spirituality? Let's go down that path.

Sid: Brave girl. Spirituality, well, I dunno if I had one really on the inside. I didn't believe in anything really of a higher nature even if I went with the flow, ya know. Christianity and all that was just there, so ya didn't really question it, you just accepted it and you kept your thoughts to yourself.

Alison: What about now?

Sid: Cor blimey, girl – now it's everywhere. Love that is, not that religious crap. Everyone goes and talks to the big cheese sooner or later. I haven't yet. I can feel all the love I need right here and as far as I know I'm made of the same stuff as him.

Alison: So do you see source as male?

Sid: Not bloody likely, nah, it hasn't got a gender but what do you call it, I dunno so "he" even if it's not he is just a term of reference. The source of all love needs no one and doesn't need a designation; we do that, that's our job so he can learn from it.

Charles: You're lucky to get such an answer from Sid, he's normally shallower than that.

Kenny: Oh yes, he is but love him or hate him, he's a good soul and we're all in this together you know, yes.

Hattie: Boys...

Alison: You do a good job, Hattie, of looking after them even now. (*It's all good natured stuff with these characters, they don't mean any of this banter negatively and I think Sid is actually a lot deeper than he's portraying himself to be here. One of the problems with channelling is that you can inadvertently give a portrayal of someone that is one-sid-*

ed – we can never know the true essence of who a spirit is because that would require us to be awake in ways we simply aren't able to be while stuffed into a 3-dimensional body. If you're wondering about the soul and if it's a singular being then that's not a correct assumption – we are multi-faceted functioning in multiple dimensions all at once.)

Hattie: They are teasing each other mostly. (*I laugh.*) You see appearances here are for familiarity of the persons they were, it's not who they are in spirit. We all swap into our highest selves but to be familiar to you and others we wear the cap of that personality.

Alison: I understand. So, Sid, have you got anything else to add?

Sid: Nope – think I've condemned myself quite nicely there don't you? 'Ere, come 'ere and give us a kiss. (*He grabs my face and plants a kiss. I can't stop laughing.*)

Alison: OK, you're a sweetheart.

Sid: You're welcome, come out for a beer when you're in my neck of the woods.

Alison: I so will take you up on that. What about you, Charles? We didn't get very in depth. Do you want to chat? (*Kenny answered instead.*)

Kenny: We all do but give yourself a break, dearie.

Alison: OK I will.

Kenny: And none of that snogging from me alright. (*We laugh.*)

Chapter 7: Charles Hawtrey and the Team

Alison: (*24 hours later.*) OK, had my break, full day, what's next, team? (*Someone is showing me black and white images of Barbara Windsor laughing.*)

Hattie: We're marshalling the troops to organise who will speak next.

Alison: Kenneth Connor came into my thoughts.

Kenneth C: Last but not least, by the looks.

Alison: I hope not, there's such a lot of you crossed over now we've got lots to get through. I always saw you as the fairly quiet one but your characters were anything but quiet.

Kenneth C: I was the smallest next to Barb that's why. Stand me next to Bernard and I'm a leaning post for his elbow. (*That made me laugh.*) No seriously, I could hide anywhere, me. (*He's a joker like the others.*) I've not got much to add to the interview really, not my thing anymore. I like the quiet life. I'm happy to let Kenny be the voice and the others too. Good gang, all of them and I really do miss those days, I really do, but I also enjoy the peace and tranquillity that not being in 3D brings with it. I love flowers and gardens and just existing in a non-hectic environment. That's me, so yes you're probably right, I'm the quiet one. I've got my books and sometimes even a pipe; it takes it out of you being human that's for sure. I was exhausted when I got here, like landing on solid ground after stepping off the waltzer at Blackpool.

Alison: Aww, OK well you don't have to be interviewed if you don't want to. I'm just really happy that you came anyway as the team isn't the team without you.

Kenneth C: Thank you for that recognition. Believe me it is appreciated and I'll hang around until your project is done and I'll join in from time to time too like I have already but shine the lights on the others if you please.

Alison: No worries, Ken – you're very sweet to come at all. OK, gang, so who's up next then?

Charles: Well I'll have another chat because you're right, I didn't finish. So where was I, can you remember?

Alison: Well I think you had spoken about your drinking and how it ruined your career in the end.

Charles: Oh it did, but I couldn't stop it. Like I said, I was a very lonely man and drink helped me cover that loneliness over.

Alison: What about the documentaries that say you were obsessed with your mother, is that a fair statement?

Charles: Mmmm yes and no. She drove me crackers but I was a mummy's boy that's for sure. I loved her dearly, bless her heart but I think she chose not to let me be a man. I was always a boy to her and of course an unmarried boy at that. Might as well let her fold my pyjamas under those circumstances because neither of us grew out of our roles like one normally would. Mumzie was Mumzie through and through. (*It's hard to really describe Charles' personality, one minute he seems quite snobbish, the other he's laid back – he's like shifting sands.*)

Alison: You had a fantastic career when you were young though didn't you? How come that didn't fill the void like it does for some?

Charles: The void was a void. It was unfillable and the older I got the bigger it got. I couldn't find comfort in love with a man, it wasn't the done thing, at least publicly and I lived in the public eye.

Alison: Was there no great love in your life at all then – ever?

Charles: There were many suitors but I just couldn't accept that was love; sex was what they brought me.

Alison: Would you change anything?

Charles: You know, probably not because the lessons were invaluable, absolutely invaluable. I certainly know where I'm going now when it comes to love.

Alison: Did you come to teach as well?

Charles: You know, I probably did. I mean it's been covered beautifully by the delightful Joan and the lesser delightful Kenny [joking] but that's what we do in a life that we entertain in. We bring people to a state of laughter to balance out the rest of it. When a lot of us thought that was hogwash, to use that term, I mean what a mixed up society that goes from accepting bisexuals (*antiquity he's referring to*) and gays as normal to turning it into the devil's work. I mean I simply can't fathom such a turnaround but we were there to bring back the capacity to love and that is duly happening now – there has to be trailblazers and we were. To look at the mess our self-images were in but we did it anyway and the worst part is that while we were in these lives, we had no idea what that role was meant for, we just existed with no knowledge of our soul contracts. We couldn't even tap into that for comfort like it can be now. When you realise that your life has a purpose no matter how dismal, it can lift you and you can possibly achieve your highest good, but to be there with no memory of that contract is well – crazy – in short. Oh I'm not complaining, I'm simply stating facts. You choose a life for yourself before you arrive then get here and promptly forget your lines.

It's like being thrown into the Harry Potter maze at the end of that movie – off you go, chaps, see you at the end for a full evaluation. By the way you won't remember a damn thing – tallyho! (*He's delightful and his sentiments ring true for me too – a little bit of spiritual memory would go a long way.*)

Alison: So then, given that position how do you feel now about society? How much has it improved in terms of the gay community?

Charles: Well a bloody great deal in the West. You can walk down the road with a same sex partner and not get arrested and there's plenty of places which accommodate gay relationships, but the marriage issue is still pending. No matter which way it gets close to the equality line, some bloody arse finds a way to drag it backwards but still it's a lot closer now than it was. You're asking in particular about Australia. (*It's a big debate at the moment here.*) Well nothing will improve there as long as the Catholics are running the show. Pseudo separation of church and state.

Alison: Yes, correct, it is pseudo separation I agree. Do you see further changes coming for the gay community?

Charles: It's like the Berlin wall. It's crumbling, darling. The cracks are showing and it will come down, it's just a matter of time and pressure. That's how this had to be seen as a diamond in the making – eventually enough pressure will create the right equality environment but white middle-class men of the religious persuasion don't like to give up their keys to the city easily.

Chapter 8: Bernard Explores the Afterlife

Alison: *We left off there for a break and restarted with Bernard. I asked the team to give me their point of view on the universe, spirituality, philosophy, God etc. to see what they would say. Bernard seems to be the hippy of the group so far.* What will you talk about, Bernard?

Bernard: The universe. You were thinking about what it means to live in a universe made by a light being of ultimate consciousness without form, 'cause it doesn't need one itself, it just is.

Alison: We're talking about source love – yes?

Bernard: Yeah, we are all consciousness, we are in a state of awareness – you know that 'cause you can feel it. That is consciousness, being able to feel, to identify oneself among the many. That's what source love is and we are derived of it. We are its avatars, its many voices. We are what makes it learn and to grow and to expand on its current state of being.

Alison: How do we do that?

Bernard: We do it experientially by having these lives we live and learning about every different way possible that there is to love.

Alison: So in my life now... I'm trying to understand why I'm here and that's about love so source can understand love? Or am I on the wrong track?

Bernard: Source is love, pure love, unadulterated by any other emotion except via the process of having many of us in an individual state to experience love of many layers.

Alison: Emotions we all have, for example, anger. Source doesn't know anger; is that right?

Bernard: Not without off-shoots of itself coming here or anywhere else really to create anger – no it doesn't without that physical experience which it can't do itself. There's no one like it to have that experience with; no second force to commune with at least on any level we understand right now.

Alison: OK so I get that source love is a pure entity of the love vibration. Why does it need to experience multiple vibrations of anger, why not just create one scenario with a couple of beings and say OK give me a play about anger? Why all the free will and memory messing when we come here? Why so many avatars does he/she need to make an anger vibration understood?

Bernard: Because there is more than one state of anger – every single scenario has a different cause. Literally, millions of ways to express anger via a vibration.

Alison: Millions?

Bernard: It's a large number and if you imagine that anger plays like a song, then by changing only one note you have a different understanding of anger. It's that complex for source love. (*He's showing me vibrating lines which change and jump about like seeing music on a computer as a visual wavelength.*)

Alison: At what point does source get to a place where it's satisfied with what it's learned about, say, anger?

Bernard: I dunno, I can't really answer that one. When you go to a shop and see shoes, not shoes but a dress you like and it comes in different colours, you want them all except they don't have it in your favourite colour. You buy the colours they have and always are in search of the colour they don't have. It's similar with source wanting to experience every possibility that can exist in the example here – anger.

Alison: Wow – sounds soul destroying when you put it like that.

Bernard: I've simplified my understanding of it, perhaps trivialized it in the process. Source has to know itself. It says I think therefore I am and then asks what does that mean?

Alison: I'm feeling more like I'm made from source the more you describe it to me. It simply wants to know its purpose just like we do. (*There's no way we could possibly fully understand the concept of such an entity in human language and so this was at the very least a surface scratcher.*)

Bernard: Yes it does and it's not an easy subject to grasp by any means.

Alison: So just tell me how you see source love then.

Bernard: For me it's very simple. I am the smaller version of source created to give experience and to also derive pleasure from having my own creator existences. I have the ability to go anywhere, do anything, feel, experience anything and then my job is done. I'm still individual yet I'm still made of source love consciousness. We get the best of both worlds so source love can experience himself.

Alison: I asked source once in a channelling what came before him/her and got strange noises that sounded like radio signals.

Bernard: That kind of info is beyond our comprehension so the answer you got, you couldn't understand it, but you got an answer.

Alison: Do you understand the answer to that question on your side of the veil?

Bernard: Perhaps not in human terms.

Alison: OK so I've got a good grasp of why we're here in the third dimension but what about the afterlife – you guys, why is there an afterlife?

Bernard: It's still experiential even without a body to control and if you go down the path of time then you know there isn't any here – there are points that represent then, now, there, here, anywhere you like, points of light that are accessed to get to you now.

Alison: So you can look at what's yet to come for us even though we think it's not happened yet?

Bernard: That's right but perhaps not so simple as until the light has been created in the future it's not fixed. It only becomes a fact once you've affected what we see.

Alison: And so time must exist in those terms; it exists for us.

Bernard: For you yes, you need time to form an organised set of events.

Alison: Can you expand on that notion because it becomes apparent that if there's no time and everything happens at once then surely all events happening can be affected to create different outcomes and again an outcome suggests that time does exist.

Bernard: You've gotta be careful you don't muddle things up here. There are many, many timelines all happening at once. I can visit you in any of your equivalent timelines and affect the outcome there. I can visit you in what you would call tomorrow; in fact I have because everything is happening at once.

Alison: Then doesn't this allow the traveller to change the future and the past in the third dimension?

Bernard: But that is not changing the future or the past as it's just another timeline that has been created. To be pure about this we should not go near what you consider your future events or your past as it creates diversions that split away by say my doing instead of your doing – I'm talking about my freewill affecting your timelines instead of you completely being random and affecting your own, but this is not a perfect universe either so this is not a problem. The issue for the world to really connect with on this level is quantum entanglement – that's what we're discussing when we talk about freewill affecting the future and the past and creating numerous other outcomes.

Alison: By outcomes do you mean creating more timelines?

Bernard: In a way yes you could see it like that.

Alison: We still have a time dilemma here because of our language being so limiting. Were you always interested in these things, Bernard?

Bernard: Not as much as I should've been. I was more of the ilk – living in the moment and I enjoyed all the moments I had. I was very lucky like that.

Alison: Do you think that is what makes a lot of people unhappy, as they're not living in the moment for all it's worth.

Bernard: This is a big one. No one on the earth right now should be thinking in terms of anything less. There's been a monumental shift in perspective yet still the human race suffers from lack of interest in their lives and they suffer for it. They think they're stuck in the mud, can't get out, and then they demoralise themselves because of it. If you're not happy with what is then change it so that you are happy. Go in search of that big job opening, or that exotic location. I know what you're thinking, that money is a limiting factor, but that is usually because the powers that be have orchestrated it so as to keep people in line. The truth is, they create their own world and the money in it. The world that is in existence for a lot of people has been created by someone else and then that leads to being unsatisfied with what they have 'cause they didn't create it. We are our own creators. If we only knew that, then things would change significantly.

Alison: You're right, the problem is fear. The human race is governed by fear both politically and spiritually.

Bernard: People have been removed from the truth that they are in control and are controlled instead – if only you knew just how magnificent you could be by self-expression and creativity but that is to come.

Alison: Well that sounds promising.

Sid: 'Ere, I want back in on that subject; it's close to my heart. I was always searching from outside for that perfect day and it never came, or should I say when it came I lost it so I felt that I wasn't in control some of the time.

Alison: But isn't that what you said in your earlier words? That you had to possess that which you loved because you were worried you'd lose it?

Sid: That's pretty much the case; self-image.

Alison: You're showing me pictures of Val...

Sid: I wasn't fair to Val; I didn't know what I had. She was my angel and I didn't see it at the time.

Alison: What would you say to her now then?

Sid: That she gave me a wonderful life and I couldn't see it for its true purpose. She was the most forgiving energy I could've asked to have with me. I needed a woman like that to forgive me of my mistakes and she gave birth to my beautiful children. Not a day goes by when I don't pop across the veil and have a look at them all.

Alison: I was going to ask you about the theatre you died in and that they say they see you there also. Is that the case?

Sid: I have been known to visit yes.

Alison: Well don't be scaring the locals anymore hey. (*Laughing.*)

Sid: You betcha!

Alison to Bernard: I'm still not getting my head around the issues you've brought up but I'll reread and try to understand what you're saying. What made you get so interested in this form of enquiry?

Bernard: I always knew that there was more to life and death than the official word stated but I was too busy with life to really get my head around any of this. It was only after I crossed that I was in a position to really delve deep.

Alison: Did you go to source love as you call it?

Bernard: I did, I was mesmerised by the expansive nature of it for what felt like an eon. Time had no meaning, it stood still. (*He's using metaphors from English to express his thoughts – our language limits us greatly in this regard.*)

Alison: Is this the ultimate of living in the moment for you then?

Bernard: You could say that. I don't really have a concept of what happened there. Imagine when you lay on the beach in the sunshine and drift away into sleep, you zone out then come around and don't even realise that your afternoon has past – gone – that's the closest I can get to describing what it felt like.

Alison: Do you go often?

Bernard: No I only went once because I understood what I needed to understand in order to continue to exist like I am and that's how I came about knowing so much about where we are. We are a balancing act of frequencies all piled together interacting with each other's dimensions and often such subtle levels that your 3D doesn't even accept that anything else exists at all but the 3D.

Alison: Is anyone else from Carry On experiencing this information like you have?

Kenny: Well I have too, been there, you know, to see him and had a different experience. My experience was a healing one. I felt quite broken when I got here, my spirit you see, my energy field, what I'm made of and I was restless with myself so I went there and came away so complete that I'm fine now. It's a popular tourist destination for spirits to go and heal and start all over.

Alison: What do any of you think now about the process of incarnating into new lives? My only way to reference any of this stuff is in linear time just in case you were going to correct me haha.

Kenny: Exhausting. Aren't we all supposed to be all "oh yes, let's jump in again"? But when you think about it; that no time exists here, our higher-self is always busy and so coming to speak with you now is part of our discarnate job. (*I really didn't understand what he meant by this at the time.*) Well we're incarnated most of the time but our higher-self can bring the life of Kenneth out and talk to you as you need me to.

Alison: Ahh, I think, yes, I get you now. Several of you when here worked on Hancock's Half Hour prior to the Carry On franchise. What was Hancock like to work with?

Sid: Big fragile ego like a lot of us. Very funny guy but easily intimidated about his role. We all got on apart from that. I loved him – funny, witty, contagious on stage, behind a mike, on TV. He knew his stuff.

Alison: Do you see him now? Is he part of the soul team you mentioned earlier?

Sid: Hancock is not going to come forward anytime soon. He made his exit and doesn't want to psychoanalyse his life. What we're doing isn't for all spirits.

Alison: Fair enough too – they have a choice as an individual. Was several of you meeting during the Hancock years destined? Did you all know there was a dynamic to be followed up with or was it coincidence that got you all into the Carry On franchise?

Sid: People in the industry know who worked well together; they saw it. They looked for it for their projects just like you are now actively seeking out the wisdom of those in the afterlife willing to come forward and teach, or tell their life stories. Same thing.

Alison: I guess what I'm really asking is did you all have a soul contract to work together given there's a soul family connection?

Sid: We did, love.

Chapter 9: Peter Rogers

Alison: *It often goes quiet in a channel session with any spirit. I call it a drop out of the line just as it may drop out on a phone call and just at this moment there was a drop out. Hattie often comes forward and tells me what they're doing. She is definitely the coordinator. I asked for guidance who was coming forward next and I start to see the producer Peter Rogers in my third eye and as yet he's not shown himself, so this is a first time and a delightful surprise that he would want to be part of this project.*

Peter Rogers, how are you?

Peter: I am very well, thank you for asking. I've been patiently waiting my turn – stepping aside so the reprobates (*jesting lovingly*) can all do what they do best and talk. What a wonderful family they are to have around me here. I am very honoured by them and of course by those who have not arrived back home yet.

Alison: So you call the afterlife home then, Peter?

Peter: Of course yes, because it is very much so.

Alison: What was it you wanted to talk about in particular or shall I ask questions? (*I wanted Peter to feel free to say whatever he needed to say.*)

Peter: Ask questions. That way, as it's your project, you get what you need out of it.

Alison: Thank you. (*He's a humbling presence.*) Well firstly I like to validate my guests. Although I know I can see a shadowy version of you as with any spirit in my third eye – I like to get extra confirmation for myself that I am indeed talking to you for my own peace of mind. It says more about my confidence than anything else if you can appreciate that – hopefully you'll be gentler than Charles was. I'm looking for indications of death, physical pains and that sort of thing. You're giving me a few different ones and thanks for being gentle. I got pain in my left side of my neck and I've got pain in my right temple and my nose feels blocked up. My eyesight is wonky on the right too. I also feel quite nauseous. I think you've covered a whole gambit of stuff there so you can pull back now please. I am satisfied that you're here with me. (*He's being ever so patient with my processes and I checked on the net but couldn't find what he died of but it feels illness related – without proof though I can't be sure so I'll just go with what he's given me.*) So while we're on the subject of dying, Peter, what was it like for you?

Peter: Well peacefully was the word. I'd done rather well with my health until that year… I remember stepping out of bed and looking back thinking oh, I'm dead: that's it and feeling it was all rather an anti-climax to die. No bells ringing, no cows mooing, no star of Bethlehem, it was all rather dull and for a while, I'm not sure how long, I didn't know what to do. I looked for a white light – felt like I was really in some kind of dream-like state. I really had to find a rational thought to explain my separation from my body then I heard calling, people calling; my mother shouting me to come. It was like I'd stepped back in time and was being called home for teatime. I recognised her, but not the scene. She stood in a bright doorway, the way she looked when I was very young with an apron on waving to me to come home. I was disoriented I must admit, still human in my thoughts but not in my body which was there in front of me and

I was floating in the air like smoke whispering around. I felt so light and free it took several moments to come to grips with the idea I was really dead. So I moved towards my mother who was waving frantically to get my attention and as I got close to her I realised whole heartedly that I was very dead but yet still alive as an essence of me – at least that thought crossed my mind at that point in time, and when I crossed through the doorway there was innumerable people waiting to greet me. I almost forgot about the life I'd simply stepped out of – so many people, or spirits rather, gathering to meet me and welcome me home and I've not looked back. I am truly grateful for the life I've had but to be here and rest is perfect. So yes this is home and home is where your heart is. My heart is here in the afterlife.

Alison: How beautiful your transition was. I believe you started your career as a reporter, is that correct?

Peter: Well yes I was very fond of current events and also very fond of writing – self-expression was how my career began.

Alison: What inspired Carry On for you?

Peter: Well, a number of things really. I like humour, comedy and I liked genre or period pieces. It was our ability to laugh at the craziness that's come before, the pomposity, the foibles of men and to a lesser degree women. I mean that sincerely because men have ruled the world and made a hatchet job of it and the women have been caught in their wake and men really are a product of their egos, always having to posture and prove their worth, yet put them in front of a beautiful woman and they become a blustering fool. I wanted to bring that out for the amusement of the audience. Don't take yourselves so seriously, that was my philosophy and that's what I wanted to portray on screen and we didn't denigrate women, we showed them in their true power and mystery or mystique. (*He chuckles quietly, he's such a passive intelligence.*)

Alison: So you wanted the audience to not take life so seriously and do it through the eyes of the postcard slapstick?

Peter: Yes and no. I simply wanted the world to laugh; that was my goal and I found the most fitting way to do that was to bring out the foibles in the people – especially the pomp – and it's in all races and all histories. The class system has no right to exist, we're all equal, all the same but we have egos which pretend otherwise.

Alison: You're showing me a video of "Carry On Up the Khyber". That was one of my favourites, I love it.

Peter: One of mine too and doesn't it just highlight what I've been saying? Look at the Governor in the big house still holding a dinner party while the place is falling down around their ears – just outrageous British pomposity. We took it to the extreme. My other favourite is "Carry On Cleo" and "Carry On Henry VIII" because we show the silly side of class and our slapstick was simply a format to laughter. There's nothing more rewarding than making a person laugh and goodness knows the Brits loved to laugh and needed to laugh. Life is hard – we delivered respite.

Alison: Do you know what drove you to feel that way about creating laughter and a respite for people?

Peter: Well I do now. It's all scripted before we get there. Our higher-self creates a set of ideals that it wishes to achieve and then we set about doing that when we're here. How we go about it, that can be random or it can be as definite as my life was; to create in the medium that I did and it was a success so we kept doing it.

Alison: So you achieved all you wanted to achieve then?

Peter: Well nothing is ever perfect but I'd say yes to that as long as you don't consider it a perfect life. I mean I would've kept on working on more films had I not checked out when I did but that was my time to go. I felt while I was there we could easily have recreated the right formula for more Carry On but in hindsight I'm no longer convinced of that. The audience's expectations have changed and sometimes the magic has gone. I now feel the magic has gone and it was time for me to leave without having created anymore Carry Ons.

Alison: So now that you've mentioned you had a good life, what was your life review like?

Peter: Well it was warm and friendly for the most part. There were certainly niggles but nothing that made me say I didn't do enough. I felt I passed with flying colours, and look, I get to spend time with some of the world's most beautiful people already here. Kenny is still such a loud one at times, the essence of him in life is still very much part of his character now. Sid, what more do you need to say about Sid? Wonderful people and I'm very honoured by knowing them all – all the faces you grew up with are here and still carrying on. There's still a lot of sentiment coming our way from planet earth. We feel it and appreciate it.

Alison: What message would you give to the world then now from your unique perspective?

Peter: Well firstly, I would say thank you for being there to support our efforts because without an audience, a movie, an actor, a producer has no voice. It's the delivery and the receiving of it that makes the success. You can't have a masterpiece with no one to tell you it is one. Secondly, I would say, don't be so serious in your life dealings, don't live in fear of change and follow your dreams. The job of a producer and entertainer is to inspire people to follow their dreams. You really can be anything you want to; you just have to have beliefs – a missing ingredient in modern culture. And lastly, no matter what you're doing, love yourself because you are the star of your own show – no one has the right to deprive you of that.

Alison: *And this was pretty much the end of the conversation with Peter – he was just lovely to channel. Very calm I felt with him and I also felt he had very strong convictions on helping people feel good about their lives through laughter as well as not taking life so seriously.*

Chapter 10: Back to Bernard

Alison: Beautiful message, Peter, thank you. What's anyone's thoughts on manifesting, as in the process of it?

Bernard: In and of itself it's a great tool to use to get what you want. We all manifested our careers.

Alison: But wasn't that predetermined by your higher-selves?

Bernard: Yes and no, the soul contract in and of itself stipulates what you want to achieve, what lessons you need to have and suggests how to go about it but all bets are off once you land in your life. For certain, we all knew we'd like to be in entertainment, but there's always an option for that master plan to go awry because of freewill, not just our own but also the will of others. However (*he pronounces it howeva*) if you travel in a soul group which we did then chances are it will go to the plan that the higher-self created. Now I can hear you thinking that sounds unfair and you're referring to money and lifestyle but remember you chose it and if you don't like it then you have to change it while you're here and that's where manifestation comes in. Most manifesters become aware of that fact during their lives and can achieve all kinds of extras to the soul contract. You can even give yourself the traits you need to come in with so that the soul has a better chance of manifesting. So it's very fair because you have to learn who you are and resolve issues and be on the lookout for clues about what you put in your contract. Take Tom Jones for example, he was born to be a rock star. He programmed all the right traits into his personality to make sure he had that experience. It was inevitable. Some will create a persona that has to work harder at it but they get there by manifestation.

Alison: OK, I getcha – so – given that some of us chose a lifestyle that wasn't meant to yield huge financial returns like my guides say I chose – how do we change that?

Bernard: It's simple, you grasp what it is you want to achieve and work to get it. Now I don't mean get a job in the local supermarket, by that I mean you plan a course of action to change your path. You need to firmly fix into your daily thoughts the changes you want to have happen. I'm looking at your timeline and you've almost always got what you wanted – it may not be about money for you though. Given that a person can't pay their bills then they've manifested that and need to change their mindset – start with a daily positive affirmation to change your soul contract and it will get rewritten by your higher-self. Our higher-selves are like politicians at times and they miss the pains of the journey like, 'cause they're not on the frontline like you are and they have a thousand other things going on. So you take the bull by the horns and you make the change for them, it will help – you're like the policy maker – so you're new policy is a fiscal one. (*He's laughing at his own analogy because it's quite clever.*)

Alison: Haha you're funny – you're good at these analogies.

Bernard: Thank you. I have my moments. Not the fool everyone thinks in the movies.

Alison: So is there a particular format to use to get the manifesting going?

Bernard: Belief. Because you came with a certain set of goals you may not have programmed the belief in so you gotta believe you're worthy for starters of a better lifestyle or job, or whatever it is you wanna manifest. Set your goals, put it out there every waking minute that you have a new soul contract going on and bring yourself a better fiscal policy that shows a surplus.

Alison: Some people say that to manifest you need to set and forget. What's that about?

Bernard: Well those are the people that programmed their lives that way – if it isn't there to start with then set and forget might mean never get. Safer to set your goals and plot a new path to get them.

Alison: Brilliant. You mentioned beliefs there and that they may have to come in with us – got any more on that subject?

Bernard: Yes – there's several ways beliefs can manifest. One is as mentioned by pre-programming the soul for the type of life it wants and the others, are by the world you're living in imposing them on you and of course by forming opinions that are completely uninformed (*or informed*). We're here to learn how to break those down. If a soul doesn't wade through these beliefs systematically it can really hinder their growth but then some of them may actually want that experience. There are no rules to this – I think you can see how randomness is important.

Alison: Yes because it really throws a spanner in the works doesn't it?

Bernard: Yes because no amount of pre-programmed soul contract and soul-character can account for randomness and anything can happen. Take Hattie for example, she came with the idea that she would battle her weight – but it didn't stop her from having a career and being thought of as a very sexy lady.

Hattie: Oh stop you're too much. (*She's grinning widely.*)

Alison: Haha he's a sweetheart isn't he?

Hattie: We love him yes he is. He's our guru.

Alison: Bernard, what do you know of how the soul personality for each incarnation is put together?

Bernard: Well it's not like a factory where you put a bit of stuff together to create an end product, although you are putting qualities together to create a personality. Some personalities you'll have noticed come out very early on in children, so a child might be solemn, or very happy and very outgoing, depending on what qualities they need to have in order to best achieve the outcomes of the soul contract. Like we all needed a fairly outgoing personality in order for us to be in the public eye.

Alison: Oh gawd I just thought about politicians – what on earth do they need? A little drop of narcissism, a pinch of self-centred, a lot of don't give a crap haha I could go on...

Bernard: Well you're not far off but it's not toil, toil, boil and bubble or summink like – it's a real art creating a personality to do these jobs, though, spirit has got it down pat these days. No eye of newt though (*he's cracking up*) and yeah you can borrow abilities from various talents and once that ability is within the soul then it becomes part of all incarnations ever after. So like you create art sometimes but it's not something you have done all your life, it came out later. The ability was there in your higher-self from another incarnation. So it stuck and you decided to access it and it took off. You found an affinity with it but I also know you've been a writer all your life and that too is part of your higher-self from other incarnations.

Alison: Ahh wow OK yes.

Bernard: Good innit? (*He smiles.*)

Alison: It's amazing and clever. So effectively then, anyone whose higher-self has ever deployed these skills, then they can be accessed at any other incarnation the lower-self has if they get in touch with their higher-self.

Bernard: Absobloodylutely!

Alison: What about protégés – what's the go with them?

Bernard: They have the soul focus on that particular skill. That's their reason for being – concentrated into one genre. For example Mozart; that was what he came here to be and couldn't be anything else like Tom Jones I mentioned earlier. It's the same for any of those personalities and they're very attuned to their higher-selves – may not know it but they do know something magical is happening when they create summink like a song or a concerto and yeah you're right in thinking there's different levels of genius, like I also said earlier about Tom Jones. (*I think he loves Tom Jones haha.*) Some souls come in with more work to do to achieve greatness in their field.

Alison: So how does the actual process work when creating traits?

Bernard: (*He's showing me a cauldron with a big mixing spoon in it and laughing.*) Literally you have access to anything you need to create the version of you to achieve the outcome for the higher-self. Your guides who you work with will help suggest to you if that personality should be shy, outgoing, and sensitive and so on. What works and what doesn't work – creating mental disorders is quite an art form.

Alison: It's starting to sound like a movie or a book project except there's room for spontaneous changes in the direction when the spirit finally puts down and lands the role in the body. How does the body affect personality – does it even have an effect?

Bernard: Oh yes it certainly does – all sorts can go wrong along the way during birth etc. but mostly environment shapes the personality after it's in the body – of course you can't predict every outcome that's just not possible given the random nature of individuality. You can know for example that the mother you contract to will have an addictive personality but you can't know what she will get addicted to necessarily. They may have contracted to be a heroin addict but learned they don't need it and stop before they have a family or they can be addicted to absolutely anything – environment shapes people after they're born. It's like you get the tool set before you're born but you don't know what you're going to make with it till you get here and circumstance may be so far off what you thought you were going to get that you can't cope and it changes everything. If you wanna be sure you're going to have a Mozart-life then you really have to plan everything to the last treble C note. (*I love his analogies.*)

Kenneth: Still boggling Alison's mind I see – wonderful. Are you enjoying this, Alison?

Alison: I am indeed, Kenny, thank you for asking.

Kenny: Well don't forget to type it up. There's an audience for this you know?

Alison: (*His fatherly tone makes me smile.*) I will I promise to keep up the typing out part – need an editor though, haha. I'm rubbish with editing.

Kenny: We're loving following you around. You're quite a personality yourself aren't you?

Alison: I'm not sure I should answer that. I might incriminate myself.

Kenny: Yes indeed – I can see you make the most of your life with little resources and I think you're wonderful for doing so.

Alison: Aww thank you, you're a big sweetie. (*He's such a cutie when he smiles – he always shows me the face he had probably in his late 20s or early 30s.*)

Kenny: Right back to you, Bernie.

Bernard: What was I sayin'? Forgot now...

Alison: Putting personalities together and seeing how they shape up.

Bernard: Oh yeah, so in terms of a politician, they have to put themselves in a certain environment growing up in order to create synchronous events – a parent who has strong views on working class joins the labour party and conditions the child like that.

Alison: What about when we see a child grow up in a poor migrant family and they do really well, like becoming a millionaire, or creating a major invention or even being a good politician. (*They must exist somewhere.*)

Bernard: Same thing – they came in with the tools and their environment shaped them. They could have had more than one door opened to go through but what you'll find is that a poor migrant family may be just the environmental leg-up a person needs to achieve greatly in their soul contract. Conversely that environment could make a person a successful criminal instead – the role doesn't really matter. What matters is that you learn the purpose of the soul contract. Many people stray off their path, such is the earth environment; it has a way of affecting healthy positive people and can ruin whole lifetimes.

Alison: I thought there were no rules.

Bernard: There aren't any – I'm talking from a human standpoint – from spirit the worst that can happen is you accidentally get killed before your time was up and so achieve nothing and even that is seen as a learning process – there really are no cock-ups, just me being a human and putting it in human terms but I guess that could be confusing for some.

Alison: Ahh OK. Hard this cross-communication isn't it? One minute you're talking from being human next from being a spirit and sometimes in between – so many perspectives and none of them are fixed perspectives, there's always room for another interpretation.

Bernard: You got that right.

Alison: Disabilities – what about people with disabilities? That's some major soul contract stuff if they rely totally on other people to get them through their lives.

Bernard: Impediments can come in any form. If you tie a baby elephant up all its life it probably won't want to try to escape as an adult 'cause it's been given an impediment. As for the highly disabled, they choose that life to learn about love no different to you and me. Look at what Professor Hawking chose to have happen to him and it didn't stop him from achieving greatness. He chose to find a way around it so his disability gave him an ability he wouldn't have had otherwise. Not all are like that I know but it's all about love and how to be loved and how to give love.

Alison: Why do they often get treated like second class unworthy citizens as if their lives are not worth anything?

Bernard: Because that brings awareness and sympathy and empathy into being and creates an environment where a person brings that emotion into the higher consciousness of people who can make changes to society.

Alison: So that then improves lives – I get ya.

Chapter 11: Joan Sims

Alison: How is everyone in Carry On Heavenly today then?

Joan: (*Giggles.*) We're wonderful, love. It's a beautiful day in paradise again. Never a dull grey day here.

Alison: And that never gets old does it?

Joan: Well you'd be surprised, Alison, because there's a need in spirits to have individual experiences and sooner or later they get the pull to go back into a body and have another crack at it.

Alison: Is that how you feel at all?

Joan: Not yet, haven't got the bug right now. I'm going to wait till earth has advanced into the new society before I go back. I want to experience a utopic future as a woman rather than come back as it is now. (*I should've asked how far into the future this was likely to be!*)

Alison: Any of the others feeling the pull to come back or are back now?

Joan: Well not as you understand it in linear terms but if you put it into our terms then we all have incarnations going on. It's a piece of our higher-self and we are both the soul and the higher-self. So that's how it works. We are co-creating for our own betterment.

Alison: I'm hearing the name Tony. Is that anything to do with you? (*She giggles but I don't get an answer so I assume it is. Names are always a challenge when channelling – I'm not sure why. Well known people it isn't 'cause we recognise them but for some reason most mediums will find it difficult to name their visitors. I think it has something to do with our own modes of blocking information out, fear of getting it wrong and so on.)*

Alison: It's been a hectic few days. Are you still with me, Joan?

Joan: Yes.

Alison: So you were telling me about the call to get into a 3D suit. Is there more to expand on that one?

Joan: Yes, yes there is. It's a call that gets stronger and stronger and it pulls you back. You can ignore it because it's intuitive and we can always ignore our intuitive feelings. It's no different than you getting the call to draw a picture or to study. It's the same thing. It's not a free-will changer, it's a reminder that if we wish to grow as spiritual beings then we have to learn as both spiritual beings and also in a 3D environment, because in that environment there are lessons that are impossible to have without a solid form. You quite rightly are picking up on giving birth to a child as one of these things. It's about love; it also can create victims and aggressive relationships which is also a learning relationship. There are so many reasons to come into a body and learn, so I'll try to explain the over-soul and the soul's appendages which is what they can be thought of as. There is the over-soul which is too large to fit into the body of pretty much any kind of being. I haven't seen one yet (*a body big enough to fit the entire soul she means*) but then there's such a vastness of knowledge, there could well be, but for now in this purpose we'll take it that the over-soul is too big to fit into a 3D body. (*She's referring to the vastness of ideas that expand into the multiverse and calling it knowledge.*) The over-soul is multifaceted; it has many facets that function in higher dimensions. In several dimensions some call it the highest part of the over-soul. The over-soul is rather like a mini version of God or source love as Bernie likes to call it. The over-soul is connected to everything. In all manners it is like a web with a core where the main thinking comes from and just like a web it has many strings reaching out into all manner of dimensions. Where we are I would call it the under-soul as we function in the 5th and 6th dimensional environment but we also reach into your 3D environment which includes time in the 4D environment. Time acts like a buffer for us, between us and on one side time is slowed to the point of laying out lives sequentially and on this side time acts like it doesn't exist as we can move around into different times in 3D by thinking our way there.

Alison: I guess I won't fully ever grasp that until I'm in the same place you are.

Joan: It's good to get a grounding of it now as it helps you understand manifesting that you asked Bernie about. You see the future is a malleable component of time.

Alison: How have you all come to learn the things you've learned?

Joan: I, like all the others, have absorbed this information in the process of my spiritual journey: when we're ready to know then we know. In earth terms I've been here quite a while yet it's barely a blink and so when we talk about our other incarnations we are referring to other parts of the over-soul because a strand of the over-soul in a body does not mean that this part of me cannot talk to you. (*She giggles again – she giggles a lot – it's lovely.*) So the spider web of the main soul is everywhere it needs to be. At any given moment there could be hundreds of threads in a different learning environment including this one on earth, also in multiple times and places.

Alison: Are there parts of our over-soul in different planetary systems then?

Joan: There can be.

Alison: The over-soul is really quite busy then isn't it? (*She giggles out the words, "You have no idea."*)

Alison: I'll take that as a yes then, haha. My next question is about the bit that you are. For example, so am I not talking to the over-soul of Joan Sims, I'm talking to the part of the soul that was Joan Sims?

Joan: Well yes and no, Alison, because I am both and I've reached out to have an experience with you as Joan Sims because that's how you know me. We can merge back into the over-soul and we often do but we can come back out again as whoever the experiencer wishes us to be (*from our soul set of incarnations*). So for example, I am a grandmother to several children in one of my other incarnations and although I have some of Joan's qualities, I also have a different set of qualities that are suitable for that role. As you know I didn't have children as Joan Sims, I had a career. That was my soul contract though I could've had children if I'd wanted but it never seemed right to do so.

Alison: Is there more you can share about that incarnation as a grandmother?

Joan: I am a traditional grandmother. I spoil my grandchild with all sorts of goodies and I'm always in trouble with my daughter-in-law for doing it but I love them and they love me and my son appreciates what I do for them so they can go have fun as a couple. I'm not married anymore and none the worse for it either, it's a happy existence.

Alison: Oh wonderful, Granny Joan, except I know you have another name for her. What does that incarnation of you think of the afterlife?

Joan: She thinks about it a lot because she is very old though not frail or fragile. I think that life will carry on living for quite some time. (*We both crack up laughing.*)

Alison: What about another life – can you share more? They're so interesting.

Joan: (*She giggles again.*) I am little girl herding sheep on a mountain in Hungary later in this century when things settle down and life for some is still very idyllic and quintessential. She doesn't have a big education but she is very connected to the land and spirit. She's a lonely child but she's never alone. She's around 15 years old.

Alison: How does, if at all, that life impact your other lives? (*This life appears to occur in our future. I wish I'd asked more about it because I simply can't wrap my head around this especially after what Bernard said – guess I'll just have to wait till I cross over for it to make sense. Dolores Cannon once described the issue of time as making a phone call from a different time-zone – both existed at the same time yet both were in different times.*)

Joan: This one is about self-sufficiency in a world where there are very few modernities. She is learning to live within herself and to feel love like that for herself as well as the environment and the animals. (*Joan is now wandering off with Bernard so I take it that we're done for the day. They're showing me beautiful tranquil blue skies and Bernard is dressed like the priest from Carry On Abroad, haha. They never cease to surprise and delight.*)

Chapter 12: Kenneth Connor – Life was a Blessing

Alison: How are you, Kenneth?

Kenneth: I'm very well thank you, Alison darling. I said I'd stay for your project and thought I'd speak a few words. I wanted to say that in terms of my life I had an enjoyable one and consider myself to be blessed. Every day was a blessing – a blessing to be alive; a blessing to be working; a blessing to entertain. I really cannot complain about any of it – I was blessed.

Alison: That's a lot of blessings, Kenneth. What inspired you as a comedy actor?

Kenneth: Well everything; the world was/is such a strange place at times. Prejudices, love, happiness, war, hate, crime, passion, and all manner of nuances, feelings and emotions spring to mind when you ask me that question: the planet earth, well, I look at it now and I wonder much – why has it got such contrast and who, what, inspires this? And I keep coming back to love. Love inspires all, whether it's through a passion we have, and a passion can come as hate – that is still love of what we stand for – so to answer your question I was inspired by the fire in my heart to give as much of myself as I could give every single day and every single performance – that's it – so simple isn't it?

Alison: That just opened my eyes wide to all kinds of ideas about who we are. I've never heard passionate hate being described as love before but you know what, that is profoundly true.

Kenneth: Am I off the hook yet?

Alison: [laughter] Not yet, you still owe me a little more, oh reluctant one – I can see you in 'Allo 'Allo now in my thoughts – just loved that role.

Kenneth: That's me, passionate about my roles no matter which one I played, actor, father, son, husband – that's why I don't need an interview after the fact because when one throws oneself into a role by virtue of love then what else is there left to say about it?

Alison: Well Kenny (*Williams*) and the others didn't seem to mind being talkers [jokingly].

Kenneth: They are the talkers – I was never a public talker. Very private – do what you do for love and let everyone else make the noise – Kenny couldn't keep quiet; on a battlefield you hear his voice.

Kenny Williams: 'Ere stop mucking abaht. [laughter]

Kenneth Connor: Have I now sufficiently filled the gap? (*What this is about is that I did Kenneth a favour by passing on some messages for him and that took away some of this chapter and so in return he came back and gave me something else to fill the gap but he really is not a talker so I'm very grateful to him for doing this.*)

Alison: Yes! Thank you for doing that you made the edit so much easier and I love your passionate philosophy about life.

Kenneth: You're very welcome, my dear one.

Chapter 13: Kenny Williams and Frankie Howerd

Kenneth: We're all here to cheer you on you know.

Alison: I feel you around me, I know you are and I'm so grateful for the support. What's time like from your perspective, Kenny? Let's have another crack at that nut haha.

Kenny: Well, you know I'm not really the one to explain that sort of thing to be honest. I've no idea how it works technically but time here is like the location you want to get to with all the boring bits cut out. So if I want to go from one room to the other I don't have to follow the path that takes time to do it. I can be anywhere at any time.

Alison: And if, say, you were following me to another room would you be there before me or would you get there at the same time?

Kenny: I would get there at the same time. There would be no need for me to wait so that means not only do I miss the bits where you have to walk, also it means the time it takes does not affect me either unless I wanted to follow you and have that experience with you.

Alison: How did that feel when you first crossed over?

Kenny: It took some getting used to I can tell you but once you do it makes you rather lazy – but then we don't need to exercise our slovenly bodies 'cause we haven't got any. We are light, bright, thought and we can do all sorts of things but because our realms are so different we tend not to mingle. I come to you telepathically into the human world because it is hard work to stay that way once you have crossed over you see.

Alison: I'm hoping that you all come for the interview when we finish the book in my lounge room space. That would be spectacular to see all your energies – maybe you will all do some funny things with the video and audio to give people the proof they need to help validate you do exist – I don't need it but many others do.

Kenny: Yes we will do that of course. That will be fun to be on the Shiny Show; you both do it so well. Very good programme for amateurs I must say. (*I think that's a compliment.*) You just wing your way to creating questions and the spirits are so impromptu – yes I like it a lot. A bit like Wogan come to think of it. (*Ahahahaha now he's mocking Terry Wogan.*)

Alison: Haha thanks – I think that's a compliment...

Kenny: Oh it is and you're both better looking than Wogan of course – you're shinier.

Alison: Thanks! So tell me what things you get up to across the veil.

Kenny: Well I very much enjoy the academia here – there's a wealth of knowledge and there's always a gig with large groups of spirits jostling about in each other's energy fields – a bit too intimate for me but I do enjoy the talks if I can avoid a huge crowd and we create whatever we want. There's no limit to what we can do, it's merely practice. I do like a good knees up though. I miss that about earth. A few drinks and a sing song – can't beat that.

Alison: Have you been to other planets?

Kenny: Oh yes, well once or twice you know I have. There's some very strange looking beasties out there indeed. Oh I went to this planet and the beings there were elephant-like, had very long proboscis noses but very peaceful race. They were in the third dimension, so like you very solid and were technologically advanced – intelligent. They didn't live in cities as you know it. They lived in the peacefulness of their nature. They walked on two legs not four and had a unique way of using that trunk-thing but peaceful – there was no exploiting their environment.

Alison: When you say technologically advanced, how do you mean?

Kenny: They had computer grids that were more like entrails across the planet, more like a biological growth – they grow them and all their waste was reused, nothing piled up and dumped in a tip. They had lots of water, jungles and so on but no waste anywhere, just this growth of networks. They didn't accumulate together like you do. They were spread out all over the place – very much in touch with the planet itself. They were not tribal but they did have a sense of community. The bio-computers were like a lifeline to each other. I don't think they evolved like humans did – it was fascinating.

Alison: I bet – I'm trying to imagine such a race. You're showing me what I would call some kind of jungle creature.

Kenny: That's what they looked like to me too. Grey skin, they didn't really speak, there was telepathy and it was a language but I understood it and they knew the spirit world was there – they weren't the least bit phased by our visit. And there was something unique about the density of the 3D because it was easier for me to condense down into it and stay there quite comfortably.

Alison: Wow! That is so exciting – I can't wait till I get back over there to experience these things as well.

Kenny: Would it confuse you to say you have already?

Alison: Erm yes (*we both laugh*) and no. I am understanding some of the concepts that are being brought to us from across the veil such as our higher-self is still there in multiple dimensions and there are many versions having lives all at once but to understand it better I should read a few more books on the subject like Convoluted Universe. I need to read that one. Have you gone up through the dimensions as well as 3D?

Kenny: Well yes and no. I tend to stay in the 5th and 6th Dimension as you understand it but I have been to 8.

Alison: Why 8 and not 7 and how do you get to 8 without going to 7 first?

Kenny: Well now that's because you see things in linear terms – 8 is not really 8, it's a density that exists alongside 7 so I don't have to go to 7 because they all are in the same space. There are dimensions between dimensions to go if you really want to get busy. There's a conduit dimension between you and me where you look into and I visit to get a better fix on you. That's what we're doing now, this is why you see us in your third eye but the reality is I'm right next to you and unless I come down with my energy even further then you won't see me. I have to make myself quite compact to be seen – that's a lot of effort if it's over a prolonged period. Your friend Erik Medhus is very good at it – one of the best. He's a fast learner and very determined soul.

Frankie Howerd: I'm being bamboozled into talking here. Not that I mind, I don't, but you know a boy has his things to do. (*He's pulling my leg and he never said who was nagging him to speak.*) So if I must I'll come have a talk. Did you know my old aunty used to wear her knickers over her frock? Mmm yes... Well I say, well... she was a little potty in the head. (*Not sure where that one was going but glad to see he's coming through, though it feels like we've had to pull teeth to get him to talk hehe and of course he's got Cilla Black with him on his arm they're having a good old chin wag.*) You know I loved my job, Up Pompeii and all that rubbish. It was a swinging good time for me and I was a bit of a swinger too if I got the chance. No point in hiding it; I loved sex as often as I could get it but with men. Everyone knew of course. I could waffle too till the cows come home. That was my stage act, to be able to gossip like an old woman.

Alison: Hahahh yes you did, you were very good at it and cheeky and saucy with it.

Frankie: Well they like that saucy humour – they did back then, made 'em feel it was OK to be naughty I think.

Alison: Have you changed your mind on the interview then.

Frankie: Ooh noooo. Still don't want to but I have to be part of it.

Alison: What shall we talk about then if you don't want to be interviewed?

Frankie: Well not much unless you're a man then we might have somewhere to go.

Alison: Ahh sorry, girly all the way here. What was it about men you preferred?

Frankie: You know I never really asked about that. I don't know, it just felt more normal. Women were these strange mysterious creatures that wanted commitments and support when I was happy in my own company for the most part. I just needed the sex part from others and I had many sex partners.

Alison: Do you realise I'm interviewing you? Hehe.

Frankie: Ooooh ... ayy ... now don't you be so cheeky, hehe. No well, alright, yes you are and if you must know I had a good life. Though many thought I was a mystery, I had nuances not foibles.

Alison: What's the difference?

Frankie: 'Ere, ooh... don't get lippy with me, my girl. (*In jest.*) You know I was shy – I over compensated by talking too much and I had a unique way of seeing how people really were so I used that in my act. I wasn't like that in my own space. I was very quiet in my own space, never said much to anyone except the four walls and they didn't care to listen either but in interviews, I felt that I was on display and had to put on my stage face. Of course people expected it and so I felt pressure to always perform and be funny. If you ask Mike Aspel and Terry Wogan and all those interview types, they will all tell you the same thing. That I was a bag of nerves and that's why. 'Cause the pressure was on always to make people laugh.

Alison: (*All went deathly silent.*) I've lost you – where'd you go?

Frankie: I'm still here giving your hand a rest.

Alison: Well you do talk mighty fast and I have to grip the pen hard to keep up with the flow.

Frankie: I know just what you mean, lovey. (*That was said in a dirty way haha but for the reader's sake I am channelling by automatic writing.*)

Alison: How deep are we allowed to go now in my quest for an interview?

Frankie: Ooh you are a right one you aren't you? Well, yes ... Ohhh no, I don't know – ask me and I'll decide on the spot.

Alison: OK. [laughs] So then, I would like to tackle the issue of sexual abuse – would you talk about that?

Frankie: Well I might. No harm no foul now I should think. But, yes I had issues with my father in that area that traumatized me and pushed me towards my mother. (*I feel as though he hasn't really looked deeply into this or if he has then he's only going to gloss the surface.*)

Alison: In what other ways do you think it affected you?

Frankie: It made me like my own company – I didn't understand anyone else. They thought I did, always tried to find out what made people tick to find out about them but I don't know if I was ever satisfied that I got all the way to the bottom of people, but I understand their behaviour.

Alison: Is that a contradiction?

Frankie: Well, I must say it sounds like it. Oh shut your face. (*He's joking.*) What I mean is: there was always the fact that when they walk away they have thoughts about you that they don't share with you but they share as gossip with others. The face they used to front you wasn't the face they really were deep down. I tried to get at that information and I never really could but I understand people well enough.

Alison: I get your meaning now.

Frankie: Ooh, you are a saucy one. Yes, I should think so I explained it well enough. (*He's always got his gossip comedic act at the ready to use.*)

Alison: So are you saying that the sexual abuse led you to being inquisitive about what made people tick, or were you going to be like that anyway?

Frankie: I was probably going to be like that anyway but it may have been a driver.

Alison: I understand. You didn't really settle down until Dennis came along. Can you talk about that?

Frankie: Dennis looked after me; he was my rock. I couldn't manage to tie a shoelace without Dennis. Broke his heart when I died I can tell you.

Alison: What was your crossing like?

Frankie: My mother was there. A beauty she was; looked like she did back in the day when I was living at home. She was a beautiful lady. Very forgiving and understanding she was. It was like another room opened up from where I was. I barely even looked at myself lying there. I thought, stupid old bugger and walked off towards my mother calling me. There were others too and I could hear a party going on in the background. Lots of noise and I thought I'm having some of that! It sounded like fun to me and so I went and crossed and there was lots of music and a welcoming home. They said welcome home, lad – time you took a break from all that. I welcomed it. I'd done all I could do here you see, it was my time and I've been very happy ever since.

Alison: Do you want to talk about your life review?

Frankie: Now there's a thing – ooh I say. Yes, didn't see that coming but all in all it was good. I got to revisit all the love that was shown me and not all of it was love; I had my battles you know, and that was not fun to relive but it was just that, a movie, so no harm no foul.

Alison: You didn't get upset by anything in it then?

Frankie: No, no, not really. It is what it is. You can't change it at that point – you are done. You learn from it. Probably that's where the most learning comes from. It's where the whole thing comes together to sum up your life.

Alison: Any regrets?

Frankie: No not a one. I lived the way I lived. It wasn't easy in those times being homosexual, you had to keep yourself on the straight and narrow, but I wasn't ashamed of what I was and I never tried to deny it to myself.

Charles: He made a better job of that than I did, I can tell you.

Alison: Thanks, Charles. Do you have another life, Frankie, that you'd like to share that had an impact on this one?

Frankie: A Russian banker I was in the 1800s – made a lot of money in that life. Shame it didn't carry over to this one though. I was ripped off greatly in this one – that might be a connection, yes – hmmm, it probably is.

Alison: This Russian banker – what did he do – family man, single, how rich?

Frankie: I was very well off. It was before the Russians revolted, before they stopped all that wealthy stuff – well before they killed the wealthy folks I mean. I had a family. I was very well-to-do. So that's the correlation from wealthy family man to poor gay man, but my life was filled with wealth as Francis in other ways you see. I had a lot of love. That was where my wealth was in this life.

Alison: And now what do you do?

Frankie: Well anything I please thank you very much.

Alison: Can you give an example?

Frankie: Ooh, errr, really, you do push it don't you?

Alison: Haha yes I try.

Frankie: Got your own way after all, my girl. I'd better watch you. (*He feels like family when he teases like this.*)

Alison: Haha yes and you love me for it don't you?

Frankie: Yes I do but don't tell anyone alright? What do I like to do? (*He's thinking out loud.*) Well I go for walks.

I enjoy even now some solitude. I have my family and we go out together to the fairs and the concerts. There's so much to do there's never a dull moment here unless you create it.

Alison: Ahh sounds wonderful. Do you travel?

Frankie: Yes I occasionally do but I enjoy my own company mostly.

Alison: So do you have anything you can share about the afterlife or your philosophy on being human – advice?

Frankie: Enjoy it. Enjoy it every day as much as you can. If by that it means you are miserable – enjoy it as much as you can. If by that it means being a drunk, then be a drunk but enjoy it. Everything you do, enjoy it. Don't whine when the wine's empty; don't complain when it's raining out and the fire's on; don't criticize others for their enjoyment, their pleasures, 'cause if you're doing that you're not focussed on your own pleasure. Being a human is one of those love-to-hate-it when they're there but blimey if you get here and forgot to enjoy being an arsehole – oh you know what I mean, no matter what your path, enjoy it because one day it will be over and you might regret that you didn't enjoy it or learn anything from it.

Alison: Thank you, that's very good advice. When you were going through your miseries did you enjoy them?

Frankie: Not nearly enough. I could've enjoyed them more. 'Ere – you giving me cheek? I've met your sort before. I'm watching you, my girl. (*He's so funny and just like having an uncle who likes to tease, you're never quite sure if he's serious or not but somehow you do work it out that he's just pulling your leg.*)

Chapter 14: Gerald Thomas, Director

Alison: Are you available, Gerald?

Gerald: Yes I am ready.

Alison: How are you, Gerald?

Gerald: I am absolutely fine, Alison, couldn't be better and I'm ready to roll with your interview. Been watching since the start of the project and I must say it's very exciting to be involved with such a thing. All too often when we pass we become forgotten on the level of still existing and I find that quite distasteful. You know we hear people thinking about us as dead and gone forever except for the legacy we left behind but how awful to hear that we no longer exist. So I am very happy to now have the opportunity to speak with you and you do seem to attract a lot of celebrities and historical figures, as I like to call them, because you're so open and welcoming to us all that we feel very appreciated from the ongoing lives we still have. I for one feel very honoured to have such a venue to speak in.

Alison: You're very welcome, Gerald. (*I feel so blessed right now.*) I'm so glad you wanted to be involved.

Gerald: Wouldn't miss it for the world.

Alison: Fantastic! So how about we start with what you're doing spirit-side since you left earth.

Gerald: Well I have to say I've been doing a little hero worship. I've caught up with some greats of my own choosing. I love Elvis and so I've caught up with him and Buddy Holly and Buddy Rich – some of my favourite people, and it's wonderful because they have such wisdom. Elvis still laughs at the campaign he was still alive, as in still on earth. (*After the death of Elvis there was a huge consortium that said he wasn't dead.*) Couldn't be further from the truth and he's having a wonderful afterlife as are we all. It's really such a pleasure to be here on the other side. We're still learning and as you say we're carrying on heavenly. There's always something to do here. Golf – I'm still not very good but I do play golf and I enjoy watching the odd bit of racing. (*Motor racing I think he meant and he is also showing me a picture of a young boy playing on a type of video game [Nintendo type game] and I can hear what sounds like cars racing so perhaps he has a grandchild or great grandchild he hangs out with on 3D-side but I've no way to verify this information.*)

Alison: From that image you just showed me I take it that you are around your family quite a bit.

Gerald: Oh yes, I am very much so, I adore being around them and experiencing their lives with them. I have three daughters altogether.

Alison: Tell me, Gerald, as I can't validate anything, it seems there's not a lot of information available about you or what your body died of. Are you able to give me a description or feelings of it? (*Here's where my own doubts come into play because I don't know how he died and can't ask anyone. I have to go with the information he gives me but our own doubts cause blockages to channelled info. I'm hearing the word "embolism" and again I can't verify that so my brain could be filling in the blanks just to give me an answer and I'm getting pressure behind my nose and my forehead as well as very hot, like sickly hot, a temperature and my head is feeling like my brain is not quite here, sort of a watery feeling. The art of channelling is a strange one where some of the information comes easily and others not so much which is down to our own insecurities.)*

Alison: What was crossing like for you? Was it an easy one or a hard one?

Gerald: Well I was feeling unwell for some time on and off but, I wasn't really focussed on dying, I really didn't expect to go. When I did pass it was a blessing. I understood that it was my time and really, I was tired and ready for it. My father was waiting for me across the veil and I looked at him with so much joy that he'd come to meet me. I felt the pull of the air around me and all of a sudden there we were standing in the beauty of the afterlife. Me and Dad just like we'd never been apart from each other. So there you have it, no guns a blazing and rip-roaring saddles of a journey across time and space, but a gentle pull to the awaiting arms of my father and we talked and talked and time stood still and I forgot that I'd died and gone to heaven for the longest time. It was reverence, absolute reverence and then I remembered what I'd left behind and felt a little sad for my family but they have done just fine without me and like I said earlier I do visit often.

Alison: What do you have to say about your film career now you've crossed?

Gerald: Wasn't that an absolute blast? The Carry On was perhaps the most fun one could ever have in life. To create such a thing that was saucy and fun to bring people together for an hour or two to laugh and wonder about who and what the actors were really all about and I know a lot of people criticized us for what we did but that's folly because these films were a rip roaring success. The everyday man loved them – our genre was to show the regular people among the gentry. (*I'm not sure I heard that part of the sentence properly.*) The rich were insanely funny to portray; I mean what they got up to was just ripe for satire.

Alison: What made you swap your career from medicine to the visual arts such as film and television?

Gerald: Well I suppose that becoming a doctor just wasn't me. It didn't feel right and I felt a very big pull towards movie making in general and so I followed my nose in that respect. It's something a lot of people don't do. They feel compelled to do what's right rather than go with their gut feelings.

Alison: Why do you think that is exactly?

Gerald: Fear. Fear of being ostracised by those that are close to them, their family and friends etc.

Alison: Fear causes a lot of problems for people doesn't it?

Gerald: It does on planet earth because fear of taking your own life in your own hands has become taboo – it always was. Parents trying to live vicariously through their children will force them into a career the child doesn't want to have. We have this insane mentality to follow or cajole others to follow us instead of taking our own power and living our own lives.

Alison: Do you think that interferes with the purpose of coming here – our soul contract for example?

Gerald: It can do, yes but also it can be the contract that we set up for.

Alison: So does a person know they're going off track then, when they do follow the path another has set for them by either parental or peer pressure?

Gerald: Follow your heart. That's the only way to do it, to know.

Alison: You have a lot of passion in that regard it feels like.

Gerald: Yes – perhaps because that's what I did – followed my heart and expressed my creative abilities. I was still a healer, I just healed by laughter instead. Not all my films were comedy though but the entertainment in general is a healing source.

Alison: What was your life review like?

Gerald: Oh it was so easy to sit through. Yes of course there were moments where I could've done better. We all have those come up in our reviews but that's our own judgement. No one else is judging us – we are our own scorer – we mark our own card. Of course there's a different vibration when a director goes as opposed to when an actor goes because the wider audience doesn't have that familiarity, but I felt the warmth and love of a great many people all the same in my review, because it showed how far and wide our work had affected people for the better more than there were people worse off for it.

Alison: Would you do anything different?

Gerald: No, no I don't think that I would. I believe I fulfilled my role on earth and I was very lucky to have a wonderful wife who took care of me so I could do what I did so well and she bore me three beautiful daughters. I was blessed every day for that alone.

Alison: What advice would you give to people then from your new perspective?

Gerald: I would tell them to follow their hearts and not allow anyone to persuade them otherwise. Your heart is your direct connection to your higher-self and your higher-self knows what it wants to achieve here. You are part of that higher-self but the human brain acts as a wall to that higher-self connection. Use your heart and you will never fail to complete your tasks here.

Alison: Thank you, that was so beautifully said. Do you have a past life you'd like to share that may have affected this one?

Gerald: Let me see. (*I can feel him thinking – this is always a strange one to express in written terms.*) I was in the merchant navy in one of my incarnations; I enjoyed the solitude of that life. I've been on boats quite a bit in several incarnations, perhaps the connection is the freedom to do my own thing there but I can't say there's anything connecting any previous lives to this one. No karma to work through. I lived my life fully as a work of art. You see, Alison, I lived my life according to my heart. I followed my desires and achieved greatly from it so that's what I mean by that.

Alison: Do you and the Carry On Team spend much time together?

Gerald: From time to time we do. We enjoy what we created while there and yes there were moments where we wondered what on earth we were doing together when we were in each other's pockets all the time but it's not like that once you cross over. Once you cross over you see things differently. You understand why this person was that way and that person was this way. Everything makes sense all of a sudden so you easily come together in love and all those issues that came about are no more. (*I'm seeing Charles in my third eye while he's talking about this subject, so I'm going to assume that Charles was one of those issues they all had while here. It's just an assumption though.*)

Alison: Do you plan to have more incarnations here on earth?

Gerald: Not in your linear terms no I don't. I'm quite happy with my golf and my Elvis music. I'm kicking back and enjoying a well-earned rest, but I have been thinking about my next incarnation. What it may entail, but we shall see.

Alison: Thank you, Gerald. You have been wonderful.

Gerald: Are we done then?

Alison: Not if you don't want to be. Keep talking all night if you like but I've run out of questions for the time being.

Gerald: Ahh I see. Well as long as I can keep talking then I shall.

Alison: Be my guest. It is an open floor now.

Gerald: Well, let me have a think about it and get back to you with some notes about my thoughts then.

Alison: OK, you're on! Anytime you want to talk I'm good to go and you can chat about any subject you like.

Gerald: Good, then it's ta taa for now.

Alison: Night night, Gerald. (*What a beautiful soul and a delight to speak to.*)

Alison: Are you there, Gerald?

Gerald: Yes I am, Alison. I was hoping to continue our chat.

Alison: I could feel you pulling on my energy gently. Haha, thank you. It was subtle so I wasn't 100% sure it was you.

Gerald: I don't want to hurt you in any way so I'm being very gentle getting your attention.

Alison: Not like Charles then when he gave me that sharp pain in my chest?

Gerald: Goodness, no but that's Charles – always has to make an entrance.

Alison: What would you like to talk about tonight then?

Gerald: Well I've been thinking and you like to talk about metaphysical things so let's try that shall we?

Alison: OK, that would be fun and I can see my buddy Bernie. That's his forte too.

Gerald: He's a good man. Our guru we call him, (*they all said this and in the same words*) so yes let's talk about the different plains of existence.

Alison: OK.

Gerald: So you live in the third dimension which consists of dimensions 1, 2, 3 and a 4th which is time. Between your 3rd and my 5th and 6th there's several other dimensions that a person can travel through but they're not really places to stay in and they flux about. They have no form that you can recognise because they are made of energy, but the energy is slightly different in each dimension. As you already know, energy is everything and everything is energy and there are different vibrating states of it, but between me and you these dimensions are a bit like mud – not quite dense like the 3D and not quite as liquid or fluid as ours. I should say stable rather than fluid. My dimensions are more stable so it's easy to reside in them. The in-between are unstable and many people in the 3D can go to them and mingle with the spirits crossing back and forth because it is indeed a super-highway of sorts.

Alison: OK I get that but what do you mean by unstable. Sounds like it could fall apart?

Gerald: Not that kind of unstable. (*He's laughing at me as if I should know my dimension stabilities much better, haha.*)

What I mean is that they flux about and are constantly changing; it's like moving around in soup. Think soup.

Alison: Ahh soup. Now you're talking metaphysical. Please continue...

Gerald: There are structures in there that resemble the human constructs but none of the laws of physics operate the same once you leave the third dimension.

Alison: That's fascinating. I know I can see into these plains or dimensions but I've only stepped on one of them once. I think the nearest one to me. It was like walking through someone's undried painting and I couldn't control my direction. There were a lot of greys and whites and then all of a sudden a beautiful being in a blue gown walked past in the distance and her gown moved with the flow of the ether like it was part of it.

Gerald: You are indeed capable of doing that yes, but many more people are opening up to it too and it does leave the world wide open to these new experiences as the veil gets thinner and the spirit realms get more obvious.

Alison: Why is that happening?

Gerald: Well, let's just say there are many things at work here and one of these is to prevent humanity from taking another tumble as previous civilisations on earth have. Yes it's very true. The earth has been populated many times by different races and the remnants of these are being discovered every day, yet the powers that be resist it because the truth is so much bigger and would turn the world on its head. The problem with trying to contain this information or compartmentalise it is that it creates an implosion of the power structures and eventually the destruction of the races that are repressed by it. So this is why the veil is coming down so that, that can't happen again. The cycle must not continue on and the collective higher-selves have made the call. It's time to introduce the human race to the galactic neighbourhood and you are one of those involved with that process.

Alison: I see – but I feel so – oh it's just little old me. Just Alison. What can I really do seriously? I'll get called a whack job. I already get called that and I've not even started yet.

Gerald: But that's OK. Anyone calling someone a whack job for doing this type of work does so out of fear of the unknown and you are delving into the unknown. However, the industry is large enough these days for there to be very many whack jobs like you so don't feel lonely on that score.

Alison: Haha, thanks!

Gerald: OK, so are we all caught up?

Alison: Yes teach.

Gerald: Good, now when a body dies, the spirit – which may have originated anywhere in the universe, another universe even a parallel dimension... etcetera has to return to the higher-self from its isolation in the physical body. The locations a soul can originate from are infinite and the higher-self was never inside the physical body in its entirety – it's simply too big for that, so it pinches off a smaller part, creates a personality, a set of ideals to experience then lets loose on the environment it wishes to participate in. Bernie talked about god or source love as he calls it, that which we all split from so we are all one being talking to ourselves experiencing all the different feelings and scenarios that are possible to exist. We're mimicking our own early existence in this way in order to learn. This too seems infinite so – on that score, souls can be born in any location of the galaxy, universe, dimension, and so the soul returns to the spirit world after the body dies and rejoins its higher-self.

Alison: That's rather a mouthful to read, Gerald.

Gerald: Stay with me.

Alison: OK.

Gerald: The purpose of source love doing this is to learn about what it is, what it can be, what it will be. Source is infinite, it never didn't exist so it's important to not try to answer that metaphysical question until one has risen up through the spiritual ranks because the answer simply doesn't make sense until you do. Just like non-linear time – that doesn't make sense while you're living in linear time. You know you cross that barrier – linear time that is – as one of the dimensions between you and me. It's one of the soups you get pulled through as you're no longer affected by it.

Alison: (*I'm wondering what flavour – no wonder I couldn't keep up in high school science class.*) What is the point to these gloopy dimensions then?

Gerald: Many. Mainly barriers that shield the spirit world from the solid dimensions.

Alison: I think you're describing the same thing that Robert Munro describes as like a grey space that's quite dense just not this dense. It sounds similar except you've put it a different way, I think he called it the m-band. When I stepped on to one of those dimensions, the one I can see any time if I want to, I felt the solidity of it under my energetic body. Clearly it wasn't solid like being in the body but solid enough for me to physically have that knowledge that something was actually there to step on to and not just remote view, and I also saw several spirits there just looking rather lost; in a state of despair.

Gerald: Of their own choosing though, that's the difference. There is only freewill. No one gets stuck anywhere they do not want to be stuck in. It is a dimension of building, rebuilding, understanding, experiencing and anything can use it for that purpose or to just be.

Alison: Ahh OK. Like a halfway house then of sorts.

Gerald: Another description, yes.

Alison: Should people fear these dimensions?

Gerald: No, absolutely not. Fear is much a human construct – a means to control the population or a means to survive a dangerous situation, nothing more.

Alison: Are there other planets that generate fear in the manner that we do?

Gerald: Yes of course. It is part of an animal's evolution to survive and fear is an instinct that we have to have in the physical setting because a life can be cut short and the lesson can be missed without fear, but also the lesson is in using that fear to survive physically dangerous situations. They happen all the time and most 3D environments have fear – it's natural.

Alison: Are there planets that operate worse than this one? More controlled, more hate, more war, more oppressions, and more discrimination and so on?

Gerald: There are those too but what makes the earth unique is the diversity, the animal variety, the plant variety and the willingness of the same humans to destroy those things for profit; to enslave animals and other humans for profit. The capacity of the human to get locked into an uncaring state is huge in this location and of course there's the complete amnesia when a spirit lands in the human body. The environment has developed into a superb training ground for the variety of emotions that can be experienced here – like a fun park with its many ways to thrill the rider. Being human has a plethora of feelings, emotions and a state of mind that can hurriedly bring a spirit to enlightenment at a fast pace. It can equally break a spirit with the same propensity and gusto.

Alison: But if there are other planets out there which are worse than us, how can being human be unique?

Gerald: The greater question is why is it so that they are unique as opposed to a world where all these things we perceive as negative are worse in nature because you are not aware of your choice to come here? Other planets allow the veil to remain open so that you can understand why you're there but earth however has been shut off and that is a means to be manipulated by forms of fear, and control has developed through the process.

Alison: You're going way beyond a personal interview. How do you feel people will accept this information?

Gerald: Many of them already are accepting of this information. The winds of change are upon us all and the process now cannot be stopped. There will be those that want to come along for the ride and a small number that won't – it's not their time and they have chosen that path before they got here.

Alison: I see. Does every single being choose that sort of thing in advance of getting here?

Gerald: Yes, yes they do.

Alison: Will the changes be gradual?

Gerald: Gradual... to morph into a society of peace and equilibrium is to turn this society on its head. The planet has polarised – there are very few who are still walking the fence in their beliefs.

Alison: Speaking of beliefs – some people will never get there until they cross over?

Gerald: That's true, but on that note it's also true that people are waking up in droves to the fact that they're being controlled by the centralised system. To say the system is democratic is a fallacy because try telling the governments they're no longer in power and see if they listen. Governments in the West have cleverly manipulated themselves into a non-egalitarian state of control – where the wealth is funnelled away from the community values and centralised into government coffers for them to choose what to do with it. Don't get me wrong, it has worked up until now, but now people are realising that they've been pulled into a type of slavery in exchange for the right to live in their own country, on their own land, on their own planet. An economic system such as earth has, takes your rights away in an underhanded fashion. You think you're free to live a happy lifestyle but try buying a campervan and pulling up wherever you like for the night. It's controlled on the assumption that you will create havoc if it isn't controlled; that's how democracy now stands. Control, because you as a citizen are incapable of controlling yourself.

Alison: Did you have a flair for unjust systems when you were here?

Gerald: I did but only to a degree. I felt that by entertainment I could kill two birds with one stone so to speak. I could help heal people with laughter and fulfil my own heart's desire to create. They worked hand in hand.

Alison: How would you like to see things change in the future?

Gerald: I see the future as a more levelled society, more community-based and assisted rather than centralised governments. The societies will be made at the local level and the community will be more help-based rather than fear-based. As it stands the community is built on fear. Lock your doors, keep your kids away from strangers, be wary of who you deal with, look after yourself first and don't care for your neighbours and such-like, but in the future it will be more idyllic and less acrimonious, but conducive to group-based living. Bartering systems and a much reduced monetary system, shared care for children and learning and so on.

Alison: What about crime? Do you see crime as an issue in the future?

Gerald: Crime greatly reduces with compassion instead of hate, when material wealth is distributed better and more evenly rather than the haves and the have-nots. Give a man bread and feed him for a day, give him the means to feed himself for a year and his community and he will be less likely to steal from anyone he perceives has more because an even distribution of wealth prevents acrimony.

Alison: Sounds a little like Communism and Socialism.

Gerald: These two political positions exploit. I'm talking about a more utopic version where violence against people no longer exists.

Alison: So do you subscribe to the more pure version of Marxism – just not the exploited version that Russia and China adopted?

Gerald: Not quite, not quite. There's room for more improvement in all that we subscribe to. Karl Marx was on the right track if you omit the revolutionary standpoint but he wasn't fully there.

Alison: Well, Gerald, I have to say you've surprised me so far. I wasn't expecting your views from the afterlife in such detail.

Gerald: I'll be back with more as long as you're up for it. A book should contain all aspects of the people it's about. Most people won't associate with this side of the director/man that I was, and that's because as a spirit I am able to see further and know more, and educate myself on many levels that is not so easily done when in a body and that's because earth is a schoolhouse for learning specific things on a personal level. Some teach, some come just to exist here and experience a human life. You know why I came but now I'm way past that life I have access to all my selves as in the knowledge of my incarnations and my higher-self as well as access to ascended beings, who have more knowledge than the size of the earth could hold – very different.

Alison: How do you envision this will take place – this transition to a new earth system?

Gerald: I see it as a slow process over time where one will become the other very quickly.

Alison: That doesn't make sense, haha.

Gerald: I know I just wanted to see if you were paying attention.

Alison: Haha, funny bugger! Well I am now. Seriously what are your thoughts or do you actually see what will happen?

Gerald: One does not see the future, one sees all the possibilities and right now the possibilities are an endless flux in all directions. The light workers of the universe are working on making these other possibilities go away – as in the ones where the earth cultures destroy themselves in a never ending karmic loop for the state of power.

Alison: Ahh I see, manifestation on a large scale then.

Gerald: Yes and it's not an easy task to create an environment where the whole planet isn't at a state of war as to the very nature of their own future. I mean we've hit a tipping point where the future will survive if it keeps up this high vibration you're all working so hard to maintain but it's such a constant task.

Alison: I've heard there will be a split in the direction of earth where we will rise up into the new earth paradigm and the other will stay low in the 3D and continue its current paradigm – is this the case?

Gerald: It is, but it's much more complicated than that. (*We took a break here.*)

Alison: (*When we got back to this point we'd had a conversation about what is to come and disagreed and this is the remainder of that conversation because I am a sceptic to certain things so Gerald was advising me to use my own logic.*) The human brain has a way of not accepting these things anyway.

Gerald: Use your own logic. I can't be real if they're not real and you know that I am. You asked me for proof and I gave it – that's your marker for a true contact.

Alison: You got me there, Gerald. Think I'm losing this debate, haha.

Chapter 15: Hattie Jacques

Alison: Hi, Hattie.

Hattie: Hello, Alison.

Alison: How are you?

Hattie: Oh I'm fine, I really am. I could feel your concern while watching some of my biography but you really ought not to worry. Yes I had my moments but the truth is, my life was full of excitement among the internal struggles of my health. I was, inside, a lost girl and my weight was a security blanket. It gave people a focus other than to look deep into me. They saw this large lady with a big smile and talent for making them laugh and I'm satisfied with that.

Alison: Oh you're right I did feel for you while I watched your bio pic but you know I grew up with you on my screen along with other greats. Diana Dors I also spoke to a while back and she had emotional battles but appreciated her life for its successes too. Tell me though, what caused you to be overweight from your teen years onwards?

Hattie: Well I'm like many other girls in that regard – I wasn't confident with who I was, what I was – I didn't have a grasp on myself emotionally growing up and there were problems in my life I didn't reveal then and won't now that are at the basis of my eating problems and self-esteem.

Alison: It's hard for me to grasp when people have self-esteem problems when they, you, were such a wonderful talent and that you were in the public eye.

Hattie: You know we soldier on and walk through life glossing over our issues instead of dealing with them. For some it paralyses, for others it makes us go out of our way to succeed. I knew I could make people laugh and I knew my place was on the stage performing.

Alison: Did you prefer any particular medium for your art; stage, radio, TV, movies?

Hattie: I loved them all. All were a way to express my talents. In a way performing is like eating, it gives you comfort. It provides from the outside what you're not capable of seeing within. We all need that part of ourselves feeding from somewhere and when we're damaged inside then the alternative is to feed your emotional self externally.

Alison: What made you drop by for an interview?

Hattie: I've been sitting back watching the goings on and thought, why not? It sounds like fun, plus some of my friends have visited mediums for a chat, why not me too?

Alison: Are you in contact with your friends from your life?

Hattie: Oh we all see each other from time to time but it's not like we're wall to wall partying. We have things we like to do here and sometimes our paths cross.

Alison: What about Erik Sykes? Did you two make up your friendship after crossing?

Hattie: It's very hard to hold on to issues you've had in the body. From here we see what conflict is really worth and it's not worth holding on to. I love Erik dearly as all my friends. He is still a very funny man – you should see him with the goons. It's hilarious!

Alison: I can only imagine, haha. It would be great to see such amazing talents hanging out together. What were the highlights of your life and career?

Hattie: Well I got to give birth to two very beautiful boys. They completed me in that regard.

Alison: But I sense something is lacking in your mood here.

Hattie: Love was lacking. I didn't fall easily into love hook-line-and-sinker like some did and I feel that was my shortcoming. Even when I did fall deeply and completely, I was let down. I felt I was not loveable truly and so I gave myself to acting and performing instead.

Alison: Do you have a relationship with your first husband John, now you're both crossed?

Hattie: I do; we will always be connected. I underestimated that relationship. I misjudged the love I had to not be a truly deep unconditional love and in doing so got swept away by someone else who was only interested in the excitement of love's first everything whereas with John, if I'd not been misled by the notion of what true love is, then I never would have broken away from John. I know that he truly loved me deeply and unconditionally.

Alison: Can you expand on the notion of love as you now understand it?

Hattie: We have an expectation that love should be exciting and always driven by excitement, that there should always be sparks flying but that's not the truth. Love can be expressed in so many different ways; we should not be restricted to only one romantic Hollywood version of it. That's not to say that there should be a lack of attentiveness in a relationship – that will always lead to feelings of lack of love but in saying that, when two people show lack of interest in each other it should be talked out honestly and then if it's agreed there is no more to be gained by staying together then it's time to leave.

Alison: Do you think that the movie industry has a lot to answer for when it comes to our notion of love?

Hattie: I do, dear, I honestly do, but in our maturity we learn that what we think is the truth can be modified by the truth of experience.

Alison: That's an interesting way to put it. Are you saying experience is the only way to find out what love really is?

Hattie: Yes I am saying that, yet all too often people don't accept that experience and still go in search of the glamour of love, which is fine if you want to chase fairytales and happy-ever-afters the movies don't portray.

Alison: Do you believe you went in search of a fairytale?

Hattie: I went in search of attention that ultimately turned out to be a front for something completely different.

Alison: Were you abused by your second husband?

Hattie: There was some of that yes. I was demanding, I wanted the excitement too. Anytime it made me feel that I was getting the notion of love fulfilled. But he lost interest and from time to time got angry with me which of course I blamed myself for.

Alison: But I'm assuming you understand that you weren't to blame for marital violence towards you?

Hattie: We see things differently yes, after we cross over and it was a hard lesson to learn during my life what love really was and I had many kinds of love to compensate for not loving myself.

Alison: What would you say to people in the same situation?

Hattie: That only they can wake themselves up out of that idea that they are the victim of love. True love doesn't come with an abusive word or a punch in the face.

True love starts in one's own heart. If you love what's inside then you will never be a victim of anyone else who loves themselves less than you love yourself. True love accepts all but doesn't accept inequality.

Alison: Are there career highlights for you as well you'd like to share?

Hattie: Well all of it was; me, my life, my soul. I couldn't have lived at all if not for performing but I think if I had to nail it down it was the Carry On era. We had so much fun creating that slapstick juvenile comedy and we developed friendships that are beyond the mortal body. I would not give these moments away for anything or anyone.

Alison: Do you have any other incarnations you wish to talk about – something that might have influenced this life?

Hattie: This life for me was so unique. Perhaps there is one other life that I used as a template but not one that overly stands out.

Alison: Is there any advice you want to give to close up with? (*I can see Erik Sykes, Hattie's comedy partner for many years looking like he wants to pipe in.*)

Erik: Hattie never gives advice do you, Hattie?

Hattie: Speak for yourself. I'm giving it all I've got while I've got an ear.

Erik: You know, Hattie, it's been a long time since we did a routine. Perhaps we should for old time's sake.

Hattie: I'm not doing a routine with you – couldn't pay me enough these days. (*She's joking.*)

Alison: Are you bursting in on Hattie's interview, Erik?

Erik: Well if no one's going to ask me then I'm bursting in.

Alison: Haha. Oh OK, what would you like to add then?

Hattie: He's bloody cheeky if you ask me.

Erik: Well I would burst in to say that I love Hattie with all my heart and that I'm sorry for my pettiness which Hattie is already aware of, but here it is again in plain text – well, in your handwriting.

Alison: Ah OK, Erik. Pop back some other time then for an interview if you like.

Erik: That's very kind of you, I will.

Alison: So, Hattie, anything to add on the wash up here?

Hattie: Yes, dear. Life is made to be in it so be in it no matter what.

Alison: Thanks I will and thank you for the advice on love. It was very insightful.

Hattie: You are welcome.

Chapter 16: Talbot Rothwell, A Last Minute Visit

As I came to the end of editing from the publisher's advice, Talbot's name kept repeating in my head over and over for a couple of days so I figured he was going to make an entrance. I reached out to him with my trusty pen and paper at the ready and here we have a brief but interesting chat with a very lovely and witty man.

Alison: Hello, Talbot, how are you? Better late than never.

Talbot: I was busy in the loo. [Laughter]

Alison: Why did you come forward so late besides the ablutions?

Talbot: Well I rather didn't want to miss out, that's the long and the short of it – a kind of peer pressure and so the opportunity at this stage of the game presented itself and here I am, dear – ready, willing and able. Talbot Rothwell at your service, madam.

Alison: Why thank you, sir – you are very kind.

Talbot: Don't let that fool you – I'm as tight as an Irishman with an orange up his arse. [Laughing] (*He's not going to be wordy here is what he's telling me.*)

Alison: Where shall we start?

Talbot: Well I always felt start at the end and work backwards was good for me but you may have another method.

Alison: With you Carry Ons it's anyone's guess. Tell me about your writing in general.

Talbot: Well in general I was a writer. It was a great escape – pun intended. Had to have something to distract us in prison.

Alison: War??

Talbot: Yes, war. Wasn't my war, I just turned up for tea and crumpets one day and next thing you know the bastards had me flying over sand and sea to visit with Gerry – nice chap – couldn't leave for months the hospitality was so good you see. [Sarcasm]

Alison: Sounds traumatic.

Talbot: Everything is on earth so you have to have comedy to make it worthwhile being there.

Alison: How would you sum up your life in a brief statement?

Talbot: Frenzied, it was frenzied – a writer's life is demand, demand, demand – oh and be funny while you are at it, chaps; don't you know there's a war on?

Alison: (*He has a very dry wit.*) So your writing career began in the forces?

Talbot: It did. I found writing within enemy lines quite cathartic, nothing better in fact. We had it better than some.

Alison: When you got home, how did the writing continue?

Talbot: I wanted it to. I'm very funny apparently – quick witted charm that's me and it worked – wooed everyone into thinking I was a genius and next thing you know we're carrying off one of British comedy's funniest carryings on.

Alison: Those two words have many connotations.

Talbot: It's pure genius – an entire comedy series linked by those two words that so accurately describes the genre. Just wonderful stuff.

Alison: Did you enjoy your life as a comedy writer?

Talbot: You know I did. Truly it was all worthwhile to have that experience and I wouldn't change a thing – not one buttonhole on Dick Turpin's coat. Nope! Every brass tack and zipper was in perfect alignment and meant to be.

Alison: Wow I love that! What was your life review like?

Talbot: Well, a bloody old movie; not that exciting but of course the love was most welcome – we appreciate those things greatly, that there are so many people who give us all the love they have.

Alison: What were your spiritual beliefs?

Talbot: Well – God was an idiot in my opinion until I got here then I realised all was well with the world. Just another Truman Show (*being crossed over allows one to see modern content so that is why he's referenced such a movie from after his death*) if you like – that really does sum this up for me. I'm grateful for my existence. I learned a great deal about humanity and about myself, my resilience, my outlook. Who I was, was made plain to me and I cannot argue with that experience.

Alison: So no regrets then?

Talbot: None whatsoever. You can never say that about your life because no matter what you did or didn't do – you stuck it out, there should be medals for that.

Alison: [Laughter] No doubt it can be implemented over your side of the veil.

Talbot: Well yes, it's a wild place in heaven and we do have a lot of fun together in our stress-free environment.

Alison: What was your greatest challenge in life?

Talbot: That would have to be imprisonment – I had to find a way to deal with it that made sense as war didn't make sense to me.

Alison: What do you think about the planet today given that you experienced war first hand?

Talbot: Well, I'd rather that it took into account war had already been and gone so why are they still at it – what's the point? I think it might be wise to say – STOP NOW! And hope that the whole world hears but of course there are those that won't and that path will continue but you're lucky you live far from it and can shut it out. I feel for those that are stuck in the middle of it. Such negativity, destruction and so on. So to answer your question – I don't think there's any value in war any more so it's time to stop it. (*He showed me images of the ravages of war while I interpreted this information, it was very sad.*)

Alison: I agree – is there anything else you'd like to say before we sign off?

Talbot: I'm glad I did this, I feel better in knowing that there's people who will read this and accept that life goes on before and after life on earth. I feel good to be able to experience that and on behalf of all the Carry On Team – bless you all – have a wonderful life. We love you, now… Carry on…

Chapter 17: Goodbye, Carry On Heavenly Team

Alison: What's up tonight, guys?

Charles: Oh, hello.

Alison: Charles! How delightful. What are you up to then?

Charles: Well I thought I'd pop in to catch up with where you're at. It looks like we're not far off done now.

Alison: Yeah perhaps. What do the others think?

Charles: It's been as strange a one for us as it has for you.

Alison: You mean the whole channelling thing – yes it is strange I guess – for me it's a challenge to get all I can through my filters and misgivings about what I do, but for you it must be something quite different. You're my childhood comedy heroes popping into my life and telling me stories. Can't beat that for a lifestyle.

Sid: Eh, what a treat. We get to watch your life with you getting to hear about ours. Aha aha aha aha, what a laugh this was.

Alison: Thanks, Sid. You were so funny and cheeky.

Sid: Don't you worry, your secrets are safe till you die apparently, aha aha aha aha.

Alison: Ha! Big teaser, hehe.

Sid: You wouldn't want me any other way.

Alison: This is true. So this is our swan song. Are we all done talking now? 'Cause I'll bloody miss you all.

Erik: Not quite. I did mean to join in but time got away from me.

Hattie: It always did, dear.

Erik: She knows me well.

Bernie: Well we thought, that's quite a bit of material for now. We can always come back and chat again.

Alison: I'm going to feel lonely without my comedy pals, and where's the most awesome Kenny – there's no swan song without him.

Kenny Williams: I'm here. Oh dear, it's like parting the waves. We're all so tangled up together now but we won't abandon you just yet.

Alison: Just yet?

Kenny: Oh you know what I mean, there's the editing and the designing and the uploading and the marketing – big job you've got. Now we'll be watching how that goes.

Alison: And don't forget the video interview when this is ready to be published!

Kenny: Oh of course not – that's the best bit. We get to be on the Shiny Show with Kari the fire cracker.

Alison: She'll love that.

Charles: Yes and make sure you do us justice when you draw our pictures for the cover art. We've been watching you think about that and we like the idea you've got.

Alison: That's good to know. You probably all helped send it to me anyway – to be honest I don't think I can do you all justice so will come up with something else.

Bernie: Well, Alison, this was quite a journey and I feel a little sad it has come to an end.

Alison: Me too; was hoping for a bit more.

Bernie: Plenty more in the pipeline to keep you busy enough for ten lifetimes. This was just a teaser to see how you went with it and thanks for caring enough about us to call us into this project. You make us feel proud to be who we were.

Alison: So you should be. You're all so amazing! [Tears]

Peter Butterworth: I'll just tag along at the end here and say it was wonderful to meet you and although I didn't join the project, I was happy to help in the end. Much of my life I'm not happy to revisit except maybe for the acting and of course my family, but I don't care to revisit the war years. But thank you for the invite all the same.

Alison: You're welcome, Peter.

So perhaps we are done then. Most of the gang popped in towards the end there to say they were done – they've given all they wanted to give on the project and now want to see it come to life as a book. I've loved every minute meeting these wonderful, intelligent spirits – being teased by them, heard the odd joke, listened to them banter with each other, tease each other and express their wisdoms from the afterlife and go to the pub with my dad. (Some of you will be glad there's a pub to go to in the afterlife no doubt.) So as for what you, the audience think about this project – well that's your journey and I hope you were enlightened and entertained along the way.

They're all waving and saying goodbye and so goodbye from me too. xoxo

Frankie: I'm always the last to know anything – bye from me and stop your bottom lip from trembling, my dear, you'll be getting all slobbery... Oh blow your nose... [Laughter]

Joan: And bye from me – thank you for letting me have such a wonderful voice. We have come to love you very much.

Alison: Awwwww now I am really going to bawl my eyes out...

Fantasy Books by this author on Amazon:
Book 1
The Aldoran Saga: Dark Hearts and dragons
Book 2
The Aldoran Saga: The Prophecy; Come the Pretender

Website:
http://www.ascendingthepath.com
Art Prints for sale:
http://alisonailfinnallan.deviantart.com/prints/
Originals can also be purchased. Please contact the author through her website for more details.